PICTURES OF TOMORROW
& RINTY

MARTIN LYNCH

LAGAN PRESS
BELFAST
2003

Published by
Lagan Press
138 University Avenue
Belfast BT7 1GZ

**ARTS
COUNCIL**
of Northern Ireland

ISBN: 1 873687 74 5
Author: Lynch, Martin
Title: Pictures of Tomorowr & Rinty
2003

Front Cover: from the Lyric Players' Theatre
production of *Pictures of Tomorrow*
(courtesy of Chris Hill Photography
and the Linen Hall Library)
Design: December Publications
Set in New Baskerville
Printed by Eastwood Printing, Belfast

CONTENTS

PICTURES OF TOMORROW

Pictures of Tomorrow was first performed at the Lyric Players' Theatre, Belfast on 14th April 1994. It was directed by Andy Hinds. The cast was as follows:

Ray	Alan Bennion
Len	Ted Valentine
Hugo	James Green
Young Len	Peter Ballance
Young Hugo	Connor Grimes
Young Ray	John Paul Connolly
Kate/Josephina	Amanda Maguire

The plays is set in contemporary north London and Spain during the Spainish Civil War.

ACT ONE

The stage is an open playing area. At centre stage, there is a light armchair, two hard-backed chairs and a coffee table. At stage right is a bay window and, beside it, an entrance leading to the hallway and a London street. Upstage, we get a sense of Spain. Golden, yellow, hot, sunny and bright. The entrance to a farm out-building is at stage left. We see olive trees. The full stage at any time can be the playing area for a London flat or Spain or both. Downstage, an elderly man enters.

RAY OLIVER is 81 years of age. He is not in the best of health. He 'carries' his left arm and walks slowly. His appearance is dishevelled. He carries a jotter and a transistor radio which he places on the floor beside the armchair where he sits. He turns the radio on.

Upstage, at exactly the same time as RAY OLIVER enters, YOUNG RAY OLIVER enters. He is 25 years of age. He is stripped to the waist and is shaving. He looks into a small mirror on the out-building wall. A young woman, JOSEPHINA, enters from the out-building, carrying a heavy box of ammunition and couple of rifles strung over her shoulder. She places them beside YOUNG RAY and exits. YOUNG RAY watches her admiringly. Presently, loud contemporary rock music is heard from the London street.

RAY: Bloody noise.

[*He hurries over and closes a window. Announcement on the radio.*]

RADIO: And now over to the BBC Weather Centre.

WEATHER PERSON: The outlook for today is mainly bright and sunny. There may be some showers in the south-east, but these should pass quickly, while tonight will be cool and dry. [*RAY is writing furiously.*] Tomorrow, rain is expected in all parts and should continue through into the early part of next week. So really, you should enjoy the sun today while it lasts. More weather at six.

RAY: More bollocks at six. [*At this, Ray's granddaughter, KATE, enters*

11

from the street. She is 26 and wearing a grey tracksuit, runners and a woolly sweater. As KATE *enters downstage,* YOUNG RAY *exits upstage.*]

KATE: Who's getting it now?

RAY: Bloody BBC weathermen. Wouldn't know the difference between a hurricane, sugar cane or Michael Caine.

KATE: Oh, you and your weather charts. [KATE *puts her bags down and begins tidying the flat.*]

RAY: That's all very well, but I wouldn't have to keep them if the BBC was even half accurate.

KATE: You don't have to keep them.

RAY: And who's gonna keep the BBC in check? Two years of charts I have there, and as soon as I get a chance to collate them, the whole lot's going to my MP.

KATE: What's the weather got to do with you? You never go out.

RAY: They're being paid public money. Look, just take this week. [*He flicks through the pad.*] Monday, they said it would rain. The sun split the trees. Tuesday, they said more rain. It was practically a bloody heatwave. Then they said the rest of the week would be sunny. And what happens? It's pissed all week—

KATE [*interrupting*]: I see the festival parade's about to begin.

RAY: Festival?

KATE: I passed the park gates just as a brilliant steel band started to play.

RAY: That's another thing. They call it a community festival. Was I consulted? Was Mrs. Bradford across the hall? Or little Paddy from downstairs? No. We're just a bunch of geriatric old bastards. We're meant to go into our beds and lie down and die for the entire weekend. Community festival, my arse. More like an excuse for terrorising the decent people of the district.

KATE: It's only young people enjoying themselves.

[*She opens a window. We hear Pogues-type Irish music and someone shouting over a microphone.*]

RAY: Enjoying themselves? People who run so-called 'community festivals' usually have a political agenda at the back of it all.

KATE: Look, we've had enough ranting and raving for one morning. Time to get ready, please.

RAY: Ready?

KATE: You know what day it is.

RAY: Yes, it's Saturday lunchtime and it's no different from any other Saturday lunchtime.

KATE: Oh yes, it is.

RAY: You're right, it is. But not in the way you think so.

KATE: Look, grandad. Both you and I have spent a long time sorting this out. We've put it off twice already. You've met the people. You said yourself they were nice.

RAY: Because they're nice doesn't mean I want to live with them. Mrs. Bradford across the hall carries my chair down to the back garden on sunny days but I don't want to lick cream off her backside.

KATE: Grandad!

RAY: I'm not moving anywhere. All I want is some peace.

KATE: You'll need some new things. A housecoat and pyjamas. I'll get them in town for you.

RAY: I never wore pyjamas in my puff and I'm not going to start now.

KATE: You'll need to. There'll be a lot of people about, including females. All there to give you their undivided attention. You met Miss McVeigh, you saw your room and you said yourself the gardens were beautiful.

RAY [*quietly*]: I'm not moving.

KATE: They're holding a reception especially for you this afternoon. All the other residents will—

RAY [*shouting*]: I'm not moving to no old people's home! [*Pause*] That's it. Final. Kaputt. [*He turns the radio on. She turns it off.*]

KATE: We agreed.

RAY: Who agreed? You?

KATE: The family.

RAY: The family? Your mother? You actually found her?

KATE: You know we rang Peter.

RAY: Peter? What's he got to do with me?

KATE: I thought he was your son.

RAY: A waster, if ever there was one. A good day's work would frighten the life out of him. And you rang him?

KATE: He's working now. On an ACE scheme.

RAY: He's 40-bloody-7.

KATE: My mum thought he should be consulted.

RAY: Why doesn't your mum come over here and consult me?

KATE: You know you always lay into her.

RAY: I've every right to lay into her.

KATE: She cries for you.

RAY: A bit late in the day.

KATE: She tries her best.

RAY: So did your grandmother.

KATE: Look, this isn't getting us very far.

RAY: Snap. And if it's okay with you, I'm expecting visitors. [KATE *is stunned.*]

KATE: What?

RAY: You heard me.

KATE: You have visitors? You haven't had a visitor in this flat in years.

RAY: I have now.

KATE: Who?

RAY: Friends of mine.

KATE: You don't have any friends.

RAY: You'd be surprised.

KATE: Grandad. This is beginning to get on my nerves. You've lived on your own since granny died, you seldom leave the flat—

RAY: Mrs. Bradford takes—

KATE: The back garden is not 'out'. You see no one from one week's end to the next, apart from me. You've had a stroke, you now have Alzheimer's, you're in need of constant professional care. You agreed you need it and I've gone to a lot of trouble to arrange it. Now, what the hell is going on?

RAY: I haven't got Alzheimer's. The doctor thinks I might have it.

KATE: Either way, there's plenty wrong with you. So what in heaven's name are you doing inviting people round here on the very day you are to move house?

RAY: What a euphemism! You call bolting me away in a geriatric hen-hole moving house?

KATE: No, but I could have you shot! [KATE *exits.* RAY *sits resolute for a moment. Then he struggles up and goes over to the suitcases. He stares at them. He angrily lifts the suitcases and empties the contents on the floor.* KATE *enters with more clothes and stops. She begins tidying the clothes in silence for a moment.*] Who are these visitors?

RAY: Old friends.

KATE: From?

RAY: The old days.

KATE: Who are they?

RAY [*irritated*]: Old friends. Comrades from the Spanish Civil War. Can I not see my old friends before I ... before I kick the bucket?

KATE: Of course, you can. But why today?

RAY: Len should have been here. The Cardiff train was due half-an-hour ago.

KATE: He's travelling all the way from Wales?

RAY: Why shouldn't he?

KATE: Where else are they descending from?

RAY: There only is another one. He's from Belfast.

KATE: My God! You're dragging an elderly man all the way from Belfast?

RAY: Not quite. He's lived in Hammersmith since 1939.

KATE: Well, at least clean yourself up before they arrive.

RAY: Mind your own business.

KATE: You won't get away with not washing in your new home.

RAY: I'm not going to any new home. And no one tells me when to wash, except me.

KATE: Your friends will smell you.

RAY: Don't talk to me about smells. They've seen me take my trousers down and shit right in front of them. And I've seen them do exactly the same. I know Len and Hugo better than their own families do. In Spain, smelling each other's smells was like reading each other's letters. A confirmation of comradeship.

KATE: You planned for this to happen today.

RAY: I didn't. Len's been writing to me for years, wanting the three of us to get together. Hugo's always on to me, 'Ray, let's get together for a drink. Let's have a reunion, sing a few of the old songs and talk about Spain. C'mon, Ray, old mate, let's get together with Len one last time?' I've always refused up to now.

KATE: So why change your mind now? What's so life-and-death about now?

RAY: There's nothing life-and-death about it. It's just that … the world has changed in the last few years. I just feel it's time for us to talk things over.

KATE: But what am I going to tell these people at the home?

RAY: Tell them … tell them I snuffed it in the middle of the night.

KATE: Alright. You meet your mates this afternoon. I'll ring the home and tell them to expect you early this evening.

RAY: You'll do no such thing.

KATE: I'm taking you in my car.

RAY: Crap.

KATE: I'm going to ring the doctor.

RAY: You can ring the Royal College of Surgeons for all I care.

KATE: It's for your own good.

RAY: Bollocks.

KATE: I'm going out now to buy you some pyjamas. I'll be back here at exactly six o'clock. You be ready and waiting.

[KATE *exits.* YOUNG RAY *enters. He lifts the box of ammunition and places it in front of the coffee table. He does the same with the rifles. He exits for a cloth and returns.* JOSEPHINA *enters with some food and coffee for him. He proceeds to eat while she cleans the rifles. At this* YOUNG LEN BUSSELL *enters, wearing a good suit and carrying a grip-bag. He coughs.* YOUNG RAY *and* JOSEPHINA *turn round sharply.*]

YOUNG RAY [*going towards him, but still eating*]: Who are you?

YOUNG LEN: Len Bussell.

YOUNG RAY: From?

YOUNG LEN: Wales. Garw Valley, South Wales.

[YOUNG RAY *holds out his hand.* YOUNG LEN *can't take his eyes off Young Ray's plate of food.*]

YOUNG RAY: Ray Oliver, London. Pleased to meet you. [YOUNG LEN *shakes, but stares at the food.*] You hungry?

YOUNG LEN: Starving.

[YOUNG RAY *holds out a piece of bread in his hand and looks at it.* YOUNG LEN *thinks it's for him.*]

YOUNG RAY: Yeah, so am I. This is our first food for 36 hours.

[YOUNG RAY *proceeds to eat it. He nods to* JOSEPHINA *to get* YOUNG LEN *some food. She exits.*]

YOUNG LEN: I've been told to report to you.

YOUNG RAY: Good. Ready for war?

YOUNG LEN [*hesitant*]: I a ... I think I'll need some training.

YOUNG RAY: You mean you haven't gone through our six-month officer training course at Sandhurst?

YOUNG LEN: I'm afraid not.

YOUNG RAY: Oh, then I'll have to put you in charge of peeling spuds and cleaning out the shitehouse. [YOUNG RAY *proceeds to open the box of ammunition.*]

YOUNG LEN: Excuse me ... sir.

YOUNG RAY: Ray. [JOSEPHINA *returns with some bread and gives it to* YOUNG LEN. *Exits.*]

YOUNG LEN: Excuse me, Ray. I know I'm not a trained soldier and all that, but I did come here to fight Franco. I wonder if you could find me some duties more directly connected to the war?

YOUNG RAY: I was only joking. As soon as we sort you out with gear, I'll book you a seat at the frontline, where you'll be close enough to pick Franco's nose.

YOUNG LEN: I didn't come here to joke.

YOUNG RAY: You didn't?

YOUNG LEN: No.

YOUNG RAY: Well, let me tell you something, Taffy. After you've spent a couple of weeks lying in the muck and shit of the trenches, with international fascism doing its level best to separate your balls from your bollocks, you'll pay good money for someone to make you laugh.

[JOSEPHINA *returns with some military clothing for* YOUNG LEN. *Exits.*]

YOUNG LEN [*apologetic*]: I thought you were trying to make fun of me.

YOUNG RAY: I was. It's called the art of survival. It's not just your skin you have to save here, you know. You've got to fight like mad to stop yourself going round the twist.

YOUNG LEN: Do I get any training?

YOUNG RAY: A week, maybe two, in Albacete. After which, we'll expect you to kill ten fascists a day. [*Quickly*] That's another joke.

YOUNG LEN: Just point me in the right direction.

YOUNG RAY: How was your journey?

YOUNG LEN: Bloody long and hard. I left home eight days ago. Told my mother and father I was going to Colwyn Bay for the weekend. I sent a letter from London telling them the truth.

YOUNG RAY: I'm sure they'll understand.

YOUNG LEN: My mother will be heartbroken. I'm her eldest son. I joined my father down the mine two years ago, but now my father's in very bad health and I'm the breadwinner.

YOUNG RAY: *Was* the breadwinner.

YOUNG LEN: I don't know how they'll manage. I feel desperately guilty.

YOUNG RAY: Well, as you and I know,Len, the fight for the Spanish Republic is more important than being a miner or a breadwinner. Fascism must be stopped here, or it will sweep the world.

YOUNG LEN: That's what Nye Bevan said.

YOUNG RAY: Nye Bevan? I wouldn't listen to too much he said. Bloody Labour Party.

YOUNG LEN: I'm in the Labour Party.

YOUNG RAY: Oh.

YOUNG LEN: That's where I heard Nye Bevan speaking. At a Labour rally in Cardiff in defence of Spain. Boy, can he speak! I never heard a man who can make you want to cry, cheer and fight all at the same time. Absolutely spellbinding. I went up to him after the meeting. I waited till most people had gone. I called him to one side and said, 'Excuse me, Mr. Bevan, but I'd like to go to Spain to fight for democracy'. He gave me the most curious look. 'This is a war, you know. It's not people shouting round corners,' he said. I said, 'I know that, but I was wondering if you knew how I could get to Spain'. He warned me against it. He told me one in three volunteers were dying in Spain and that I should go away home and think very carefully about it. I said, 'I'm sorry, Mr. Bevan, but I've given it all the thought I need. I want to go to Spain'. A week later, I was on my way.

YOUNG RAY: To Colwyn Bay?

YOUNG LEN: God forgive me.

YOUNG RAY: This bloody ammunition! Three-quarters of each box is useless.

YOUNG LEN: How did you get to Spain?

YOUNG RAY: Very simple. I was working as a compositor in Fleet Street when the party put out the call for volunteers. I applied immediately.

YOUNG LEN: The Communist Party?

YOUNG RAY: Of course. Joined when I was 16. The week after the General Strike, 1926. After I watched my father sit down and cry because he couldn't feed his family.

YOUNG LEN: How did your people take it?

YOUNG RAY: Oh, great. They're both in the party now. They've been great. My biggest problem was tearing myself away from Rachel Prescott, the most beautiful girl in the whole of London. Think she's quite upset that I'm here. [*He instantly pulls out a photograph of a girl and shows it to* YOUNG LEN.]

YOUNG LEN: She's very nice, very nice indeed.

YOUNG RAY: She's beautiful. Thinks I'm totally batty. Doesn't know what Spain's got to do with me. But—I haven't told anyone—we got engaged the day before I left.

YOUNG LEN: Congratulations. It must be love.

YOUNG RAY: She writes to me twice a week. Even sent me a hat she made, with my initials embroidered on it. [YOUNG RAY *shows* YOUNG LEN *the hat.*] She says if I wear it into battle, I'll never be shot. [YOUNG LEN *has selected his clothes.*] Get what you need?

YOUNG LEN: I think so.

YOUNG RAY: Right, over to your billet. I'm putting you beside an Irishman. Eamon Downey, the poet. He's a fine young fellow, but he never shuts up. And when he should be fighting, he's writing bloody poetry.

[*They are about to move off when* YOUNG LEN *accidentally drops his helmet. He picks it up and looks at it, a little nervously.*]

YOUNG LEN: Is it true? That one in three volunteers are dying?

[YOUNG RAY *looks at* YOUNG LEN, *looks away and back at him.* YOUNG RAY *smiles.*]

YOUNG RAY: Who's counting? [*He goes over to* YOUNG LEN.] At this very moment, the biggest battle since the Great War is raging at Jarama, just outside Madrid. Franco has publicly declared he wants the capital urgently. He's getting very close. He's hit the bar a few times. He's got German planes, German pilots, Italian soldiers, Moroccan soldiers, Portuguese, Spanish, all running at the Madrid defence. But they haven't scored yet. All the British and Irish boys have been in the thick of it. Some have died. Some of us have survived. But nobody's counting.

[YOUNG RAY *exits.* YOUNG LEN *stares after him. We hear loud music as* LEN BUSSELL *enters from the street. He stops beside* YOUNG LEN.]

LEN: Heavens, that music's loud. [YOUNG LEN *exits.*]

RAY: No, it's not. It's great fun. The festival committee says it's great fun. [RAY *closes the door behind him, fading the music.*] No problem finding the place?

LEN: No. Taximan knew the district well.

[LEN *is 78 years of age, An ex-full time trade union official, he is still a fit, sprightly man. He is dressed very neatly with an overcoat, suit, shirt and tie, brylcreem on his hair, etc.*]

RAY: Take your coat off. Sit down. Hugo will be here very soon, so I'll leave the tea till he comes, okay?

LEN: Fine with me. But will Hugo want tea?

RAY: Hey, it's good to see you, Len. It's incredible, but you've hardly changed since I last saw you.

LEN: You must be joking. I'm 78 and I feel a hundred and eight.

RAY: You're talking? I was two hundred on my last birthday.

[LEN *takes out a pipe.*]

LEN: Mind if I smoke?

RAY: Len, you were a devout Methodist, didn't smoke or drink.

LEN: I started this after we lost the last miners' strike.

RAY: You said something in your letter about meeting your daughter in London?

LEN: Yes. I thought, since I was coming up to see you and Hugo, I'd take the opportunity to visit my daughter.

RAY: I'm sure you're looking forward to it.

LEN: Can't wait. It's really silly. It's been a long time and I've two grandchildren I've only seen pictures of.

RAY: You'll enjoy that.

LEN: They're meeting me at Putney Bridge tube station at eight o'clock and I'm staying the night with them. They're making a big thing about my visit.

RAY: Well, it is good to see you, Len. It really is.

LEN: And how have you been? I can't say you haven't changed. 1968? Almost thirty years ago.

RAY: You made a pretty good trade union leader. I've seen you on TV a few times.

LEN: With my face washed, I hope.

RAY: I haven't always been in the best of health, Len. I had a stroke a couple of years ago and, only a fortnight ago, my doctor confirmed I'm at the early stages of Alzheimer's Disease.

LEN: Christ! I'm sorry to hear that, Ray.

RAY: My granddaughter, Kate, looks after me.

LEN: Your granddaughter.

RAY: Well, she's more like a daughter, really. Marion and I have raised her since she was ten.

LEN: You've had your hands full.

RAY: She's been away at university, but she's back working in London now. Last month, she had to come and collect me from Fulham football ground. I was found sitting at the players' entrance with an autograph book. I don't remember a thing about it.

LEN: I really am very sorry to hear that, Ray. But why do you keep going back to see Fulham? They hadn't won anything when you were in Spain and they still haven't. [RAY *smiles.*]

RAY: At least we have football teams in London. What have you got in Wales, only rugby teams and male voice choirs?

LEN: Don't you start Hugo about the Welsh.

RAY: What's the chances that the first thing he shouts when he comes through that door is 'manos arriba!'

LEN: Yeah, manos flaming arriba. [*Mimics*] 'I was the only man never heard them words. I wasn't captured.' [*The men are laughing.*] Hugo was the biggest liar I ever came across.

RAY: He loved trouble, didn't he?

LEN: Loved it.

RAY: In fairness, he hated Franco. I never came across a braver man in Spain. Hugo was my Alan Ball.

LEN: *Alan Ball?*

RAY: In every great football team, you need certain types of players. A great goalkeeper, a midfield ballplayer, a goalscorer. But you also need a worker. Somebody who'll run and run, cover every blade of grass and win balls. The type of job Alan Ball did for England in the 1966 World Cup. Hugo was my Alan Ball. Volunteered for everything.

LEN: Do you remember the time General Lister visited us at the front?

RAY: Didn't Hugo shake hands with him or something?

LEN: Shake hands? He volunteered a plan he had for killing Franco. He wanted permission to surprise Franco while he was having Holy Communion and slit his throat.

RAY: Pity it never came off.

LEN: It still annoys me to think that Franco, the man that started it all, lived into his old age and died peacefully in his bed.

RAY: Unlike many of the young men who went out with us.

LEN: Like Eamon Downey. Do you remember his beautiful poems?

RAY: Of course I do.

LEN [*reciting*]: 'As my spirit spirals forward seeking strength,
I catch myself painting pictures of tomorrow.'
Downey-the-poet the boys used to call him.

RAY: Yeah, yeah, Downey-the-poet.

LEN: He was such a smashing fellow. Wasn't he, Raymond?

RAY: Eamon was my midfield artist. My Bobby Charlton. Always brimming with ideas. Always in the thick of things, prodding and poking the opposition, but never losing his composure.

LEN: And who was I in your great Spanish football team?

RAY: You? Nobby Stiles.

LEN: Nobby Stiles? I wasn't anything like Nobby Stiles.

RAY: He was the heart of the '66 team. The hard man. Quiet off the field, but a tiger on it.

LEN: I was shit scared most of the time in Spain.

RAY: When you arrived, yes. You were the shy little naive village boy from the Welsh valleys. But we all soon found out what a tough, stubborn little bastard you could be.

LEN: I have a great memory of you in Spain, Ray.

RAY: Always complaining about the coffee.

LEN: My one great memory of you, and this is leaving aside all the great, very brave things you did as our commanding officer, I will always remember you singing 'Mack the Knife'.

RAY: What a ridiculous thing to remember.

LEN: I'd love to hear you singing it again, Ray.

RAY: I can hardly breathe now, never mind sing.

LEN: How long is it since you've seen Hugo?

RAY: A year ago. At a Communist Party function. He's always on the phone. But I haven't been able to get about much since the stroke. Look at my bloody arm. [*He holds up his arm. It shakes.*]

LEN: So, you're still a committed party member after all these years?

[RAY *shakes his head slowly.*]

RAY: No.

LEN: You never mentioned any of this when I wrote to you.

RAY: I didn't see the point.

LEN: This is quite a shock. I expected you to be one of the diehards, Ray. In fact, I was talking to Hugo just last year and he assured me you were a fully paid-up party member.

RAY: I still am. Unbroken membership since 1926.

LEN: So what are you talking about?

RAY: I'm paid-up. But my heart hasn't been in it in recent years. The Berlin Wall coming down was like one of those slow-motion dreams you have, where you're falling from a high building and you're powerless to do anything about it. When the Soviet Union collapsed, I hit the ground and was able to watch my skull splinter into a thousand little pieces. All in slow motion. I've given up, Len.

LEN: I never thought I'd hear you say that.

RAY: Listen. I stuck it out, right through Hungary, 1956. I remember feeling uneasy about Czechoslovakia in 1968, but I believed it had to be done. The doubts were shoved well to the back of my head. But now, now even the Russian people have rejected it. It's all come to a very, very sad and confusing end.

LEN: You've told the party?

RAY: No, I haven't. And I'm not going to.

LEN: You must have been to some meetings?

RAY: No. I've been able to use this [*Holds out his shaking arm*] as an excuse.

LEN: This is … this is quite incredible, Ray. If you've stopped believing, you have to tell them.

RAY [*sharply*]: No. No, I can't.

LEN: For your own sake.

RAY: I can't walk away after all these years. It's been my whole life. Every day for sixty years, I woke up, I thought 'Party'. Every friend I had was in the party. I even married a Communist. There's been nothing else. I had no life whatsoever outside the Communist Party. I was on the national executive. I was a hero of the Spanish Civil War. I'm looked up to by thousands of party members. I don't want to let all those good people down. I don't want to betray anyone. I haven't got the courage to walk away.

LEN: Does Hugo know this?

RAY: No.

LEN: Are you going to tell him today?

RAY: You mustn't say a word, Len.

LEN: You haven't even discussed it with him?

RAY: Are you mad?

LEN: Surely, even he'll understand.

RAY: Len, Hugo loves me. And I think the world of him. But he's a dyed-in-the-wool old Stalinist. He's as active now as he was when he joined. It's a bit like watching Alan Ball still trying to cover every blade of grass at Wembley thirty years after the event.

LEN: Always trying to recapture his youth.

RAY: Sometimes I'd give anything to be 19 again. To get all the old certainties back.

LEN: In your younger days there are no contradictions. When I first discovered socialism, I wanted to pass it on to every man, woman and child.

RAY: When I first read Marx, it warmed my heart. It was beautiful to read. It took a little German Jew to make me first understand who I was, who my people were. He explained why there was the haves and the have-nots. He even told us who was to blame.

LEN: All we had to do was work out how best to change things.

RAY: That's when it got tricky.

LEN: I joined the Labour Party.

RAY: I definitely didn't join the Labour Party.

LEN: But we agreed on Spain.

RAY: Everybody agreed on Spain. That's why men and women from all over the world came to join the International Brigade.

LEN: They came from 53 different countries. The most unusual army ever assembled in the history of the world.

RAY: But I don't want this to sound sentimental or stupid, Len, but … I have always been proud to know you.

LEN: And me you.

RAY: No, I mean this. Me, you and Hugo, we went through so much together.

LEN: So why did you never agree to us getting together before this? [*The front doorbell rings.*]

RAY: That must be Hugo now.

LEN: I'll get it, Ray. [LEN *exits. Upstage, it is night-time. The silence is broken by the distant sound of* YOUNG HUGO *singing* 'The Internationale'. *It gets louder.*]

YOUNG HUGO [*off-stage*]: 'So comrades come rally
And the last fight let us face

The Internationale
Unites the human race ...'
[*He enters, gesticulating, bottle of wine in hand, shouting.*]
Viva la Republic Espanya! Viva la Communist Party! Where the
hell is Eamon Downey? Viva la Pasionaria! [*He shouts, punching
the air.*] Viva la Republic Espanya! Viva la Communist Party! Viva
la Pasionaria! [*Looks around*] Where the hell is Eamon Downey?
[*At this,* JOSEPHINA *enters. She furiously remonstrates with* YOUNG
HUGO *in Spanish.*]

JOSEPHINA: Callarte tu boca, estas haciendo demasiado ruido, callarte.

YOUNG HUGO: What?

JOSEPHINA: Que estrepito tranquilo hombre!

YOUNG HUGO: Listen, love. I got expelled from Slate Street School
when I was nine. I can hardly speak English, never mind Spanish.

JOSEPHINA: Por favor, no cantar, los militarios estan intentado de
dormir. [*The girl grips* YOUNG HUGO *and tries to take the wine off him.
He, in turn, grabs her and tries to dance with her. She fights him off.*]

YOUNG HUGO: Viva Irlande! Viva the Falls Road! Viva Leeson Street!
Downey, come out wherever you are!

JOSEPHINA: Por favor, un fochito de silencio ya estas!

YOUNG HUGO: 'So comrades come rally
And the last fight let us face ... '
[*The girl slaps* YOUNG HUGO *hard on the face, just as* YOUNG RAY *and*
YOUNG LEN *emerge half-dressed from an out-building.*]

YOUNG HUGO: What the ... ? [*He grabs the girl and begins shaking her.*]
Who the hell do you think—

YOUNG RAY: Right, right, right, that's enough.

YOUNG LEN: Easy on, easy on. [*They separate the fight.*]

YOUNG HUGO: Did you see what she did to me?

JOSEPHINA: Estas imborracio, demasadio ruido.

YOUNG HUGO: She slapped me on the face, the bitch.

YOUNG RAY: I take it you're Boyd, from Belfast?

YOUNG HUGO: It doesn't matter who I am, but who does this bitch
think she is?

JOSEPHINA: Tienes que este en la cama, hay una guerra sabes.

YOUNG HUGO: Yeah, and up your arse, too.

YOUNG RAY [*firmly*]: Okay Boyd, that's enough. Over there, and I'll
talk to Josephina.

YOUNG HUGO: Over where? Who do you think you are?

YOUNG LEN: Listen, mate. This is Ray Oliver, your commanding officer.

YOUNG HUGO: Ah, Christ, no. You're Ray Oliver? Ah, Jesus, I'm sorry, mate. Sorry, sorry about all this. I was supposed to be here earlier. I'm Eamon Downey's mate from Belfast.

YOUNG RAY: Okay, move off.

YOUNG HUGO: Right, right. [YOUNG LEN *guides* YOUNG HUGO *across stage.*] Who is that witch anyway?

YOUNG LEN: That's Josephina. She cooks for us. [*To* JOSEPHINA] It is okay, I'll deal with him.

YOUNG HUGO: I'm not eating anything she cooks.

YOUNG RAY: Gracias. Muchas gracias.

YOUNG LEN: You'll eat every bite she puts in your mouth and be glad of it.

JOSEPHINA: Make sure he goes to sleep.

YOUNG RAY: It's okay. [JOSEPHINA *turns to go.*] Buenas noches.

JOSEPHINA: Buenas noches. [*She exits.* YOUNG RAY *joins the others.*]

YOUNG RAY [*to* YOUNG HUGO]: You need coffee.

YOUNG LEN: I'll make some. [YOUNG LEN *exits.*]

YOUNG HUGO: I am very sorry, Mr. Oliver. I didn't mean to waken everybody up.

YOUNG RAY: I'm Ray.

YOUNG HUGO: I'm Hugo. Hugo Boyd, Falls Road, Belfast.

YOUNG RAY [*pointing to* YOUNG LEN]: He's Len. So, why did you not arrive along with the rest of the recruits?

YOUNG HUGO: It wasn't my fault, I swear to God. In Barcelona, our train was delayed and when it come, it was jam-packed with refugees running from the fascists. I mean, absolutely jam-packed. There was no way I could get on it. Honest to God, I tried.

YOUNG RAY: How come the other 44 recruits were able to get on it?

YOUNG HUGO: I'm reporting that crowd. Who do you make a complaint to around here?

YOUNG RAY: About what?

YOUNG HUGO: Them other recruits. They trailed women and children off that train to get on it. I saw women hurt and crying.

YOUNG RAY: So what did you do?

YOUNG HUGO: What could I do? The bloody train went without me.

YOUNG RAY: You were left on your own?

YOUNG HUGO: Completely and absolutely on my Jack Sloan.

YOUNG RAY: You contacted the International Brigade headquarters?

YOUNG HUGO: Not straight away.

YOUNG RAY: Why not?

YOUNG HUGO: Well there was an anarchist office beside the train station, but I wasn't going in there, right? Next door to that,

there was a ... let me find a polite way of saying this ... a
whorehouse. But as a principled communist, I couldn't let myself
darken its doorway, right? [YOUNG LEN *arrives with the coffee.*]

YOUNG LEN: Why not?

YOUNG HUGO: It was bloody well closed. Then, next to that was a pub.

YOUNG RAY: A pub?

YOUNG HUGO: Now, you have to consider the situation. I had been
travelling since I left Belfast 14 days ago, with strict orders not to
draw attention to myself in England or France, in case the
authorities stopped me coming here. No talking to strangers, no
socialising, no drinking. I hadn't a drink in 14 tucking days.
That's the predicament I found myself in.

YOUNG RAY: So you succumbed?

YOUNG HUGO: No, I did not. Not immediately. But as I entered that
pub I heard music. Flamingo music.

YOUNG LEN: Flamenco.

YOUNG HUGO: Flamenco, whatever it is. As soon as I walked in the
door, there was two of the ... ooh, the finest looking women I
ever saw, doing Flamingo dancing.

YOUNG LEN: Flamenco.

YOUNG HUGO: By God, it's stirring stuff, isn't it? The two of them
came straight over and started dancing with me!

YOUNG LEN: You enjoyed yourself then?

YOUNG HUGO: Enjoyed myself? One of them didn't want to let me
go. Senorita she said her name was. She wanted to take me back
to her house and stay the weekend. I says, 'Senorita, nothing
would give me greater pleasure, but I'm a Belfast communist on
my way to beat the bollocks out of Franco and mere matters of
the flesh will have to take a back seat.'

YOUNG RAY: You left, then?

YOUNG HUGO: Not at that exact moment.

YOUNG LEN: Why not?

YOUNG HUGO: She took me upstairs.

YOUNG RAY: What about fighting Franco?

YOUNG HUGO: Fuck Franco! A man in need will temporarily shed
the greatest cause at the sight of a good pair of tits.

YOUNG RAY: Well, the cause is still very much here. And you need
some sleep to prepare for it. [*They get up to go.*]

YOUNG LEN: Six o'clock start in the morning.

YOUNG RAY: That's four hours away.

YOUNG HUGO: Why, what's happening?

YOUNG RAY: We're going on the offensive at Brunete.

YOUNG LEN: Franco will not be amused.

YOUNG HUGO: Franco? Will he be there? In person, like?

YOUNG RAY: Could well be.

YOUNG HUGO: Good, good, good. Tell the Vatican to prepare for Franco's funeral. What sort of weapon will I be getting? Put me in charge of a tank so that, when I aim, I won't miss his big, fat, ugly, stinking, fascist, Catholic, Nazi, pea-brained, baldy, Spanish nut.

YOUNG LEN: Well, I don't think you left anything out.

YOUNG HUGO: I did. He's a big-nosed glipe as well.

YOUNG RAY: Hugo. Sleep. [*At exit*]

YOUNG HUGO: Right, right. Sleep. By the way, where's that reprobate Downey?

YOUNG RAY: Leading the advance party, the Yanks and the Canadians.

YOUNG LEN: By the time we rise, Downey'll be in the thick of it.

YOUNG HUGO: Did I not tell you about the time me and him went—

YOUNG RAY: Sleep, Hugo!

YOUNG HUGO: Yes, yes, right, kip. Some shuteye.

[YOUNG LEN *and* YOUNG HUGO *exit, while* YOUNG RAY *finishes off his coffee. Off-stage, we hear a commotion as* YOUNG HUGO *discovers his sleeping quarters.*]

YOUNG HUGO: What? I'm supposed to sleep in that?

YOUNG LEN: It's fine. You'll get used to it.

YOUNG HUGO: Used to it? It's a friggin' barn. Kane's Rag Store wouldn't be in it. I'm going back to the Flamingo dancers in Barcelona. Who could teach me how to dance Flamingo?

[LEN *and* HUGO *are in the hall out of view. There has been a dispute and the men are shouting. They enter.*] Where's the nearest pub to here?

YOUNG LEN: Will you shut up, Hugo!

HUGO: It wasn't my fault!

LEN: Hugo, will you shut up!

[YOUNG RAY *exits.*]

HUGO: I'm not letting him away with that.

LEN: Shut up, Hugo.

[HUGO *is 78 years of age. He is carrying a crash-helmet under one arm and a haversack on his back. He wears a dark brown suit, shiny and worn, a white shirt open at the neck and a black beret on his head. He is extremely agitated.*]

HUGO: That bastard punched me.

LEN: You hit him first.

HUGO: He deserved it. He nearly knocked me off my bike.

LEN: It was an accident. Wipe that blood from your mouth.

HUGO: Blood? Right, I'll show the bastard—

LEN: C'mon, sit bloody well down.

HUGO: It's alright for you, Len, you weren't punched by a six-foot lorry driver.

LEN: Forget it, Hugo.

HUGO: I'll remember his face.

RAY: This is typical.

HUGO: What is?

[*The others sit down while* HUGO *remains standing. He generally prefers to stand or pace about than sit.*]

RAY: Always in trouble of some sort.

HUGO: I didn't start it.

RAY: You're an old man now, Hugo.

HUGO: What do you mean?

RAY: I mean, the next time you attend a funeral, you'll be exempt from carrying the coffin.

HUGO: Who? I'm as fit today as I was when I arrived in Spain in 1937. How are you, Ray, old mate?

RAY: Fine, Hugo. [*They shake hands.*]

HUGO: Good to see you, Len.

LEN: And you too, Hugo. [*They shake.*]

HUGO: I walk five miles every day, drive the moped to Brighton once a week and I'm available any time the wife feels up to it. Which isn't very often. Here, that was a nice wee woman I saw on the stairs there.

RAY: Mrs. Bradford.

HUGO: Nice pair of legs.

RAY: That's my neighbour you're talking about.

HUGO: Well, invite her up.

RAY: She's too young for you. She's only 68.

HUGO: Good, an unwanted pregnancy won't be an issue then.

RAY [*attempts to get up*]: Right. Lunchtime, gentlemen. I'll put the kettle on.

LEN: Sit where you are, Ray. I'll put the kettle on.

RAY: Thanks, Len. First on the left.

HUGO: Kettle? I thought this was a reunion of old comrades. Where's the drink?

RAY: Tea first.

LEN [*moving to exit*]: Don't tell me you're still a boozer, Hugo?

HUGO: No, I gave it up. I only drink now at weddings, funerals, christenings, Holy Days of Obligation, all public and bank holidays, Christmas, New Year, Easter, Valentine's Day, Father's Day, Mother's Day, St. Patrick's Day and every Tuesday and Saturday. No, I gave up drink as a bad job years ago. [*He laughs.* LEN *exits to the kitchen.*]

RAY: Still the same old Hugo.

HUGO: Still the same old Hugo. Only younger.

RAY: Fag?

HUGO: I'll have one of my own roll-ups, if that's okay. [RAY *lights a cigarette.* HUGO *lights his.*]

RAY: Thanks for coming.

HUGO: Don't mention it. But this is the last day of the British Open. I could be watching it with the lads in the pub. [*Takes an swing with an imaginary golf club*]

RAY: By the way, I'll get you a drink soon, but let's take it easy. You know what the vicar's like.

HUGO: I'm alright with the fags, Ray. I really don't care much for drink these days.

RAY: Well, Jesus, I do. Don't leave me on my own. I just don't want to chase him away.

HUGO: Remember the time we spiked his drink in Gandesa?

RAY: Shshush.

HUGO: He walked up the village main street in his underpants. [RAY *and* HUGO *try to suppress their laughter.*]

RAY: Then he tried to kiss Josephina the cook. [*More laughing*]

HUGO: Oh, right, before I forget. [HUGO *takes a long brown envelope out of his pocket and hands it to* RAY.] This is for you.

RAY: What is it?

HUGO: The conference in Birmingham.

RAY: Hugo, you know I'm not fit.

HUGO: I'll arrange for a car to pick us two up.

RAY: I can't afford to go.

HUGO: What do you think that is? The party sent it. Your expenses and something extra for the bevvies.

RAY: Hugo.

HUGO: The party needs you in Birmingham, Ray. It's going to be a crucial conference.

RAY: I can't take this.

HUGO: Instructions. No argument. Bert wants you there.

RAY: How is Bert?

HUGO: Same as ever. A cantankerous wee shite.

RAY: What's that smell?

HUGO: Len's burnt the toast.

RAY [*sniffing*]: No, it's not … toast. It's a strange smell.

[HUGO *holds out his cigarette.*]

HUGO: It's a … it's probably this.

RAY: What is it?

HUGO: It's only a wee bit of Bob Hope

RAY: Drugs? Jesus Christ. Hugo, you're the only man I know who immatures with age.

HUGO: When I was 21, my da said to me, 'Hugo, son, life is short. Try everything at least once, except religion and sheep-shagging'. Unfortunately, I only discovered dope ten years ago.

RAY: Say nothing to Len.

HUGO: Ach, he should a been a bishop instead of a trade union leader. Doesn't drink, doesn't use bad language, doesn't look at dirty books and believes the Labour Party is socialist. Huh.

RAY: I'll give you this, Hugo, your mouth shows no sign of slowing down.

HUGO: I told you, there's no part of me slowing down. I'm like the Royal Family. I'll keep going till I'm found out.

RAY: Your health's been good, then?

HUGO: Haven't been to a doctor since I got married. 1942.

RAY: What about the wife?

HUGO: It's a lovely sunny day, isn't it?

RAY: Yes, but—

HUGO: We're expecting to have a nice, pleasant day today, right?

RAY: Of course, but—

HUGO: So why do you have to mention my wife?

RAY: But you're still together?

HUGO: In much the same way as China and America sit on the same United Nations Security Council.

RAY: I thought she might have left you by now.

HUGO: Who? A river can't leave the mountain. How is it you start off a marriage with all these things in common. Live side by side for fifty years and end up the only thing you have in common is the fact that you're married to each other. I suppose it might have been different if she could've had children.

RAY: Marion's been dead three years.

HUGO: You always were lucky.

RAY: Hugo, my wife was an alcoholic. She made my life hell.

HUGO: I always told you, shoulda married that girl you went with before Spain. Rachel somebody.

RAY: She married a solicitor.

HUGO: She deserved that. No. I wouldn't wish that on any wee girl.

RAY: My life might have been so different with Rachel Prescott. No, I know it would have been different.

HUGO: You've only wasted fifty years of your life. It coulda been worse. Just imagine if you had had a great life, everything you wanted, happy and contented. Would you want to go? Would you be ready to pop off without complaint? Not at all. This way, with a messed-up life, you'll be happy to get it over with. [*Mimics, holding his hands on his chest*] 'What's this, pains in my chest? Great, take me, take me!'

RAY: Are you ready to go?

HUGO: Not until I've slept with a black woman. [*Laughs*] What about you?

RAY: Strangely enough, no.

HUGO: Probably because you think you'd bump into your alcoholic wife.

RAY: I thought that ... when I reached the ... the ridiculous age of 80, there'd be no problem. I'd go whistling, cheerfully. But that's not the case at all. I don't want to go. I do not want to go. Okay, I'm 81, I don't have an 18 year-old body, but I'm okay. I feel fine. Who says I have to go?

HUGO: You're yapping. Waffling. Give it a rest and pour yourself a drink.

RAY: My granddaughter wants to put me in an old people's home.

HUGO: Oh.

RAY: Old people's homes are for old people.

HUGO: Do you know what we need? We need a drink.

RAY: Yeah, you're right. [LEN *enters.*]

LEN: Here we are, nothing like a good cup of tea.

RAY: Oh, fantastic.

LEN: What's all the shouting been about?

HUGO: It's him. He doesn't like old people.

RAY: I didn't say that. I just don't want to live with them 24 hours of every day.

LEN: Who says you should?

HUGO: His granddaughter. She wants to put him in an old people's home.

LEN: When's all this supposed to happen?

RAY: Today.

LEN: Today?

RAY: She has it all arranged. She called here earlier to pack my bags and take me in her car.

LEN: And?

RAY: I threw her out.

LEN: Good for you.

HUGO: I thought as much. It's not like you to let anybody jump all over you, like, is it? That's not the Ray Oliver I knew.

RAY: She's coming back.

HUGO: When?

RAY: Six o'clock this evening.

LEN: What for?

RAY: To take me to the home.

HUGO: So. Throw her out again.

RAY: I agreed last week that I'd go.

HUGO: So? You changed your mind.

LEN: You've told your granddaughter that you don't want to go? [RAY *nods*.]

HUGO: Right, that's it. We'll be here when she comes and, between the three of us, we'll 'repel the attack', right, lads?

LEN: I'm sure she'll listen to reason and understand.

RAY: Unfortunately, she's a bit like myself. Headstrong.

HUGO: Well, we kept Franco's army out of Madrid, we can beat off Ray's granddaughter. Let's have a drink and draw up the battle plans. [*He takes a bottle of whiskey from his haversack.*] Just for you, Ray, old mate.

LEN: Isn't it a bit too early in the day for drinking, Hugo?

HUGO: Well, when Jesus was turning the water into wine, it was only the ones who turned up early were able to get drunk. Who wants a Black Bush?

LEN: You're a terrible case, Hugo.

HUGO: Any glasses?

RAY [*pointing*]: In the kitchen.

LEN [*exiting*]: For God's sake.

HUGO: Here, I forgot to tell you. I've been invited to Barcelona.

RAY: What for?

HUGO: Ach, just one of my old girlfriends wants me to meet my grandchildren. [LEN *returns. The men laugh.* HUGO *pours drinks for himself and* RAY.] Len?

LEN: No. I'd take a beer, if there was a beer.

RAY: In the fridge.

HUGO: One-beer Len. Watch you don't get drunk.

LEN: No danger. [LEN *exits again.*]

RAY: He's meeting his daughter at Putney Bridge tube station at eight o'clock. He can't turn up smelling of beer.

HUGO [*shouting*]: That's what's wrong with the Welsh. Dylan Thomas died of drink and he's a national disgrace. We made Brendan Behan a national hero before he was cold in his grave. All the same, it must be sad for the Welsh. They produce one good writer, *one* good writer, and he drinks himself to death. The Irish could afford ten Brendan Behans.

RAY: Who's produced more writers than England?

HUGO: England? Apart from Shakespeare, who I admit was a good minor playwright, the only writers to come out of England were Spike Milligan and the guy who writes *Only Fools And Horses* for the BBC. Both of Irish extraction, I might add.

RAY: I grant you, the Irish do produce good writers.

HUGO: More writers per square inch than any country in the world.

RAY: Because you had nothing else to do. [LEN *enters.*]

LEN: The English were too busy building an empire.

HUGO: Well, I'd rather sit in a house writing a poem than go around raping and plundering half the world.

LEN: Ireland's a place where half the population sits around writing self-pitying ballads and the other half travels the world singing them.

HUGO: Oh, you two are ganging up on me now?

RAY: You started it.

LEN: We're only retaliating.

HUGO: Well, I never heard the words 'manos arriba'.

RAY AND LEN: Here we go.

HUGO: In two years in Spain, I never came close to holding my hands up.

RAY: We didn't give ourselves up.

LEN: We were captured. [HUGO *'covers' them with an imaginary rifle, prowling around them.*]

HUGO: Manos arriba! Manos arriba! Hands up! You dirty, Commie International Brigaders! Manos arriba! Que hace usted aqui?

RAY: We weren't fast enough to avoid capture. Every time there was the smell of danger, you were away like the clappers.

LEN: Jessie Owens the second.

HUGO: In war, two things determine a great soldier. The ability to hold on to your smokes and the resolute determination never, *never,* to be a hero.

LEN: You were wounded more times than us.

HUGO: Yes, but if you check my medical records, you'll see all my injuries were inflicted from the back. Back of my left arm, back of my left heel, back of my thigh … I was running away every time!

LEN: While we stayed and fought.

HUGO: That's why you ended up in Burgos Prison and I didn't.

RAY: Cut the codology, Hugo. You were a bloody good soldier. You were my Alan Ball.

HUGO: Alan Ball was a tube.

RAY: He was not.

HUGO: He was like a headless chicken running up and down the pitch. All legs and no brain.

RAY: You were Alan Ball.

LEN: I was his Nobby Stiles.

HUGO: If I was anybody out of that team, I was Bobby Charlton, the midfield general.

RAY: Rubbish.

HUGO: Okay, at least … at least … I was Bobby Moore.

RAY: I was your commanding officer. I was Bobby Moore.

HUGO: What about the goalscorer, Geoff Hurst?

RAY: No.

HUGO: Martin Peters?

RAY: Alan Ball! You were Alan Ball, and you should be proud of it.

HUGO: Well, at least Alan Ball was a better player than Nobby Stiles.

RAY [*winking at* HUGO]: Shut up and pour yourself another drink.

HUGO [*feigning*]: Ah, no. I couldn't … well, only if you join me.

RAY: You wouldn't get us some water, Len, please?

LEN [*standing*]: I am not going to stay here while you two get drunk.

HUGO: We're heroes of Spain. We deserve the odd drink. The man's not all that long out of Burgos Prison.

LEN: Who? He was only there a weekend. I was two years in Burgos. [LEN *exits.*]

RAY: In 13 months, I killed seventeen thousand, five hundred and sixty-six lice in Burgos.

[HUGO *pours more whiskey, including a large portion into Len's beer.*]

HUGO [*as they laugh.*]: We'll give him a Gandesa. It must have been terrible. You two lying tucked up in your beds, while I was fighting the last losing battle of the Ebro.

RAY: Yes. You did cover yourself in glory.

HUGO: I was a good soldier.

LEN [*returning*]: We were all good soldiers.

RAY: Do you remember the first time the three of us fought together?

LEN: The Battle of Brunete.

HUGO: July 6th, 1937.

RAY: They had us up at six o'clock in the morning.

[YOUNG LEN *enters, buttoning up his jacket.* YOUNG HUGO *enters. He is irritated and still only half-way through dressing and snatching bites from some bread.*]

YOUNG HUGO: Frigging disgrace, getting men up at this hour.

YOUNG LEN: Raring to go, Hugo?

YOUNG HUGO: It's sleep I need. Why can't they organise the war so that you get a good sleep and a good lie-in in the morning? That way, we'd be in a better state to fight.

YOUNG LEN: Why don't you go back to bed?

YOUNG HUGO: Who? I'm looking forward to this.

HUGO [*looking at* YOUNG HUGO]: I was like hell. Standing there that morning, I don't think I've ever been so terrified in my life. I'll always remember the sun that morning, shining deep, hard into my eyes, like it was telling me 'Right, Boyd waken up, this isn't the Falls Road, this is the real thing. This is Spain. All your joking and drinking and flamingo dancing is over. Pick up your rifle.'

[YOUNG HUGO *picks up his rifle. He looks at* YOUNG LEN.]

YOUNG HUGO: How are you feeling yourself?

YOUNG LEN: Perfect. At last, the Republic's going on the offensive. We can now start pushing them back. I'm excited.

LEN: Excited? I was so scared, I couldn't sleep a wink all night, couldn't eat any breakfast. I hated the waiting, the hanging around. It gave you time to imagine what your brains would look like splattered across some field.

HUGO: At that very moment, I couldn't think of anything else but Belfast. In my mind's eye, I was walking down the Falls Road, waving to people I knew in Royal Avenue. I was watching the people of Belfast on their own streets. The dockers, the shipyard men, the poor millworkers, the unemployed, the wretched. It was them I was there for. At that moment, I would have given anything to be among them.

LEN: As I stared out over the straight rows of olive trees, all I could think of was the Brecon Mountain in South Wales. When I was 15, that was the first mountain I climbed with my mother and father on a Labour Party ramble, 1931. And I remember looking across at the lorry waiting to take us to Brunete, and all I could see was my mother and father, sitting on the lorry, kissing and cuddling. Then my mother started handing out sandwiches to some French volunteers. I remember her face was so beautiful. So sad. I had betrayed my mother, and even in the biggest battles, her face was always there. Like it was tattooed ten feet in front of my eyes.

[YOUNG RAY *has entered. He is reading a letter.*]

YOUNG LEN [*smirking*]: Another letter from Rachel.

YOUNG HUGO: 'Dear Raymond, Piss Off. I've found a tall, dark, handsome, obscenely-rich lover.'

YOUNG RAY [*embarrassed*]: A letter from the party in London, actually. More recruits on the way.

YOUNG HUGO: Uh ah. [YOUNG LEN *laughs.*]

YOUNG RAY: Are you men ready?

RAY: You didn't know it, Hugo, but it *was* another letter from Rachel. A month before, Eamon Downey and I had got locked into an argument about commitment. I had confided in him how much I was missing Rachel. He was appalled. He said if I was a true communist, if I was serious about defeating Franco, I should break off my engagement to Rachel. He said the revolution doesn't need any girlfriends. You knew Eamon—he was so fanatical, so brilliant with words. I wrote to Rachel and broke it off. The letter you saw me reading that morning had me close to tears. Rachel was distraught. I really wanted to cry. But all around me was … was this war. Men with guns, tanks loaded with shells, the smell of war was everywhere, and then, in front of me, were you lot. And I was your commanding officer. It was bizarre. Of course, I hated Franco. It was just that I loved Rachel Prescott more. I thought about saying a few words to the men, but … but all I could do was sing.

[YOUNG RAY *begins to sing* 'Avanti Popolo'.]

'Avanti popolo, a la roscosa
Bandeira rosa, bandeira rosa
Avanti popolo, a la roscosa
Bandeira rosa, triumphera.'

[YOUNG RAY *continues to sing, softly.*]

LEN: It was the right thing to do at the right time. Your singing sent shivers running down my back. God, I might have been scared but I was proud to be there.

HUGO: When the singing started, my adrenaline started pumping. I was ready for anything.

LEN: I remember the exhilaration as I watched the other men board the trucks, Germans, Dutchmen, Chinese—

HUGO: Russians! An absolute babble of languages!

LEN: All fighting together for the dignity of man!

HUGO: For an end to poverty!

LEN: Democracy!

HUGO: People all over the world declared their support for the Spanish Republic.

LEN: Hemingway visited!

HUGO: Orwell fought! [YOUNG LEN *and* YOUNG HUGO *join in the singing.* HUGO *and* LEN *are now almost shouting.*]

HUGO: Pablo Neruda spoke out!

LEN: Paul Robeson came to the front and sang!

HUGO: Brecht demonstrated!

LEN: Sean O'Casey supported us all the way!

HUGO: The workers of the world were, at last, truly united!

LEN: Fascism would be routed!

HUGO: Franco defeated!

LEN: Kill the bastard!

LEN and HUGO: Salud! No pasaran!

[*At this, the young men start another verse of* 'Avanti Popolo', *this time louder. With rifles raised, they march on-the-spot, stamping their feet to the rhythm of the song. At the same time,* LEN *and* HUGO, *with fists raised, march up and down past each other, singing along with the young men in a rousing, climactic celebration.* RAY *remains in his chair. As* HUGO *gets carried away, he jumps up on a chair near the exit, punching the air with his fist. The song ends sharply, as* KATE *enters and looks up at* HUGO.]

KATE: I thought the Spanish Civil War ended years ago.

Black-out

ACT TWO

Ray's flat. KATE *is standing with her coat on and her arms folded. She is doing her best to contain herself.* RAY *is seated and drinking.* LEN *is seated and puffing on his pipe. All eyes are on* HUGO, *who is in the middle of the floor, physically demonstrating a theory of his.*

HUGO: What I'm saying is, anyone who comes near you, anybody you see in the street, each of us in this room, we're surrounded by containers.

LEN: Containers?

RAY: You're definitely going off your head.

LEN [*looking around*]: There's no containers around me.

HUGO: Invisible containers. They're not meant to be seen.

RAY: But you can see them?

HUGO: Anyone can see them. If you look, if you really get to know someone.

LEN: What do you mean by containers?

HUGO: They could be anything. Wine bottles, black plastic bags, china tea cups, milk churns, plastic cups, anything.

RAY: And what's in them?

LEN: Is there supposed to be anything in them?

HUGO: Yes, yes, of course. That's what it's all about. They contain everything that we keep private about us. I call them our Horseshit Containers.

RAY: Thank God old age hasn't affected me like you, Hugo.

HUGO: I'll give you an example. See me? Look at me. Look closely. Just above my left shoulder, here, there's a little tube of toothpaste, right. This small tube—actually, it's family-sized—this tube holds all my hatred for my da.

RAY: Your dad's not still alive?

HUGO: He died in 1959.

RAY: So, what the hell?

HUGO: You tell me. I've tried. I've worked hard to forget, but he hurt me at a most important stage of my life and I can't get that out of my head.

LEN: Was there a big falling out?

HUGO: Yes.

RAY: When?

HUGO: 1935.

LEN: Boy, you hold a grudge.

RAY: And you never made up?

HUGO: Sort of, yes. We were 'okay' when he died, that's why it's only a tube of toothpaste and not a beer keg. [*Moving swiftly on to* RAY] Now, take Ray Oliver, 81-year-old Spanish Civil War veteran, anybody, anybody with eyes in their head can [*Physically demonstrates*] see this sitting directly on top of his head. [*To* RAY] Your hair needs washed.

LEN: What is it?

HUGO: It's a beautiful little Chinese Ming vase. Beautifully patterned, little delicate handles on each side and a nice little lift-off lid.

RAY: What do you think's in it, Hugo?

HUGO: Rachel Prescott.

RAY: Rachel Prescott?

HUGO: And your other women.

RAY: My other women? [RAY *laughs out loud. He takes a good laugh.*]

HUGO: Watch, Len, don't lean over too much to your left. You'll knock over that lemonade bottle beside your shoulder.

RAY: Fifty years of Welsh mistresses!

LEN: I've only had two! [RAY *and* LEN *laugh.*]

HUGO: It's pound coins, actually.

LEN: Ohhh!

RAY: I always thought you were a repressed capitalist.

HUGO: I don't think you ever got over Rachel Prescott, Ray.

RAY: A lemonade bottle full of pound coins.

HUGO: You've always said you messed up with her.

RAY: Shut up, Hugo.

KATE: Grandad? [RAY *looks at her.*] Can we talk?

RAY [*sharply*]: No.

LEN [*getting up*]: Come on, Hugo, I think we should head off—

RAY: No. You're my guests. I want you to stay.

LEN: We'll go outside for a bit of fresh air. See what's happening in the street.

HUGO: The gassing of the old age pensioners doesn't start till eight.

RAY: Nobody's going anywhere. This is my flat, my party. Stay where you are. Hugo, pour out the whiskey there. Len, take a drink?

LEN: The beer's fine with me.

RAY: Good, good. All we need now is for my granddaughter to take herself off home and let us get on with our drink. Right, lads?

KATE: Right lads nothing. The three of you are pathetic. [*Silence*]

RAY: Get out! Get out, Kate! I don't have to put up with this.

KATE: What is going on here? I mean, what is going on here? I don't know you two men, but I really don't know why three elderly men are sitting round getting drunk when one of you is practically an invalid and is meant this weekend to be sorting out the rest of his life.

RAY: Without your help, thanks.

HUGO: If only I was drunk.

LEN: If you don't mind me saying, dear, and I know it's turned out a very awkward time, but I haven't seen your grandfather in nearly thirty years. We were only enjoying a little get-together.

HUGO: We came through a lot together, before you were even born. You might not be aware of it, but your grandfather was a great man. A hero of the Spanish Civil War. You need to show him a wee bit more respect.

KATE: I love him because he's my grandfather—

RAY: You've a funny way of showing it.

KATE: —not because he fought in some war. I don't even know when the Spanish Civil War was. The 1920s, 1930s? Who cares?

HUGO: We care.

KATE: Good for you. I care for the here and now and what's going to happen to him.

LEN: What do you work at, Kate?

HUGO: Are you blind, Len? She's a Grade A yuppie. 'The here and now'. 'I'm alright, Jack'. This is one of Thatcher's children, Len. They don't give a toss for man nor beast. Probably spends her week with her feet up at a computer, when she's not swanning in and out of fancy wine bars.

KATE: I'm a social worker, if you really want to know. And if spending eight hours a day, every day, on the worst council estates London has to offer is some sort of qualification for yuppiedom, I'm the Duchess of York.

LEN: You do care, then?

KATE: About my work, yes.

LEN: But you don't run a business.

KATE: I like my work.

LEN: What do you believe in?

KATE: I believe no one should be hungry, abused or homeless.

HUGO: You're talking socialism.

KATE: No, I'm not. I'm talking Africa, the Third World.

LEN: So why should you work in London?

KATE: Because there is hunger, abuse and homelessness in London. But if you want to argue over politics, what you should argue over is black starving Africa.

HUGO: And I suppose you're a Green freak as well.

KATE: I've talked it over with Miss McVeigh at the home and we think we have a solution. Just give me five minutes?

LEN [*stands up*]: C'mon, Hugo. Let's go down and get that fresh air.

HUGO: Right. I haven't had a good dance since Nelson Mandela got out of jail. [*They move to exit.* HUGO *passes near* KATE.] Watch that heavy black bag doesn't fall down on top of you. [*She doesn't reply.* HUGO *gets to the door.*] All that sexual repression.

[*The two men exit. We hear loud Waterboys music as the men exit.*]

RAY: Your grandmother fucked me up. Your mother disgraced me. What are you trying to do?

KATE: And you're nothing more than a poor put-upon victim.

RAY: I didn't deserve what I got.

KATE: Didn't you?

RAY: You have no idea.

KATE: Don't I?

RAY: You're not much more than a child.

KATE: I have heard stories.

RAY: What? The incoherent ramblings of stupid women?

KATE: They call it their side of the story.

RAY: Kate, listen to me. You have no idea. You have no idea what it's like to come home at four o'clock in the afternoon, after a hard day's work, and find your wife sitting in the kitchen half-drunk. To find a glass of vodka hidden under the sink and empty beer tins in the bin. Do you know how devastating that is?

KATE: Why did she drink?

RAY: Jesus Christ! Why is there salt in the sea? Alcoholics don't need excuses.

KATE: I'm not talking about excuses. I'm talking about reasons.

RAY: There's no such thing.

KATE: I'm not so sure.

RAY: What are you talking about?

KATE: I know about your other women.

RAY: What? You're not listening to that fool Hugo? That was just a joke.

KATE: No. I was listening to my grandmother.

RAY: Drunk, no doubt.

KATE: Maybe. I used to think that probably it was the ramblings of a confused, embittered woman. Hugo's Ming vase just makes me wonder.

RAY: That Ming vase stuff was nonsense.

KATE: Grandmother told me about the women in your office.

RAY: Huh, that again.

KATE: Bernie Mooney, the Irish girl. [*Pause*] The Blackpool lady.

RAY: These are figments of your grandmother's imagination.

KATE: You didn't have to flaunt your indiscretions by bringing them to your local pub, taking them on holiday.

RAY: Kate, your grandmother was paranoiac. Any woman I ever spoke to—

KATE: Do you know what it's like to sit at home, night after night, not knowing where your husband is? Who he's with?

RAY: You don't know. You just do not know. You're like the cop who arrives at the scene of a fight and arrests the person who is retaliating. You don't know all the facts.

KATE: My mother told me she used to come down the stairs at night to find gran sitting crying her eyes out.

RAY: Oh, so you're invoking your mother now. The woman who abandoned you when you were ten years old.

KATE: She's still my mother.

RAY: Someone should have told her that.

KATE: Who is Rachel Prescott?

RAY: That was way before I even knew your gran.

KATE: Who is she?

RAY: Does it matter now?

KATE: Hugo seems to think it does.

RAY: That's his opinion.

KATE: What's yours?

RAY: Look, if you want to know about Rachel Prescott, I'll tell you. She was my first girlfriend before I went to Spain. We finished while I was out there. I came home and met your gran and that was that. End of story.

KATE: Did you love Rachel?

RAY: No ... not really. Maybe, at the time, but ... it didn't last long.

KATE: It doesn't sound like that to me.

RAY: I've had enough of this.

KATE: Hugo says you messed up.

RAY: Could I be left alone please?

KATE: Well, just don't come crying to me, ever, ever again.

RAY: You don't know half the bloody story. Now, go home.

KATE: I'll tell you what I'll do now. I don't ever want to hear you talking about gran's drinking again. Not until you've put your hand on your heart and asked how much you contributed.

RAY: Alcoholics are born, not made.

KATE: Well, maybe if gran hadn't had to go through her life trying to be Rachel Prescott, she wouldn't have needed drink.

RAY: Nobody needs drink.

KATE: Nobody needs hypocrites.

RAY: Out!

KATE: All the women in your life ever wanted was some love and you couldn't give it to them because you married the wrong woman. Honestly, I feel so sorry for you.

RAY: Out!

KATE: I'm going. I did come here to try and persuade you, again, to move to where you can be looked after. And as from now, I don't give a fig whether you stay here or emigrate to the mountains of Andalucia! [*Exits and slams the door behind her.*]

RAY [*shouting*]: Come back when you know the whole story! [RAY *leans back against the wall, tired and reflective.*] I wish to hell I was back in Spain!

[YOUNG RAY *enters. He has a piece of paper in his hand.* YOUNG HUGO *and* YOUNG LEN *enter. Grim-faced, they meet, shake hands and embrace.* YOUNG HUGO *is particularly distressed.* YOUNG RAY *addresses the men.*]

YOUNG RAY: The front is being threatened in three or four different places and this unit has been ordered back into the line. I know this is a particularly difficult time for all of us. Eamon Downey's been sharing our lives for over a year now. He was more than just a comrade. He was a dear friend. A young man just 22 years of age, an earnest young man, a man of great intellect despite his young years. And a poet, a poet of enormous potential. We all remember his insatiable appetite for debate, his constant striving to define what we mean by communism and socialism. He often talked about his native Belfast. About the poverty of the people he grew up among. And their children. That's what drove him on. His vision of the future, the next day, tomorrow.

We lost other good men we all knew and fought with. Their deaths only serve to strengthen our resolve. Fascism will not win. We have the responsibility of the entire workers of Europe, to make sure it doesn't win. No pasaran!

I took this off the field kitchen wall. It's a poem written by Eamon after his first day's fighting at Jarama. [*He reads*]
'The morning dawns on straight rows of twisted olive trees
As taut, silent men assemble.
Idyllic waters from afar pour over me
Quenching thirst, feeding fear.
Wild berserk thoughts warm up, bend,
Then break and float away.
As my spirit spirals forward, seeking strength,
I catch myself painting pictures of tomorrow.'

YOUNG HUGO: Again. Again, read it again!

YOUNG RAY: 'The morning dawns on straight rows of twisted olive trees
As taut, silent men assemble.
Idyllic waters from afar pour over me
Quenching thirst, feeding fear.
[*The three men shouting.*]
Wild berserk thoughts warm up, bend,
Then break and float away.
As my spirit spirals forward, seeking strength,
I catch myself painting pictures of tomorrow.'
[*Bombs go off. The young men throw themselves on the ground and take up firing positions. Ray's living room. Elvis Presley singing 'Surrender' blares loudly. The room is untidy now, with coats, beer-cans, glasses of drink, ashtrays, cups etc, strewn around.* LEN, *with his shirtsleeves rolled up and tie removed, enters dancing across the room with an imaginary partner. He sings along with Elvis. The music ends.* LEN *heads for his drink.* RAY *looks at his watch.*]

RAY: Listen, Nobby. It's now twenty past eight. Aren't you even going to phone your daughter?

LEN [*empties his glass*]: Screw my daughter.

RAY: You're leaving her standing at Putney Bridge tube station.

LEN [*pouring himself another drink*]: She left me. I didn't leave her.

RAY: This is most unlike you, Len.

LEN: I have my pride.

RAY: At least slow down on the booze.

LEN: You're sounding like my wife.

RAY: You're behaving like my wife. I love to see you enjoying yourself, but I don't like the idea of your daughter standing at a tube station waiting on you. The girl will be worried.

LEN: Worried? That page is missing from her dictionary. She wasn't worried when she ran off to London seven years ago and never contacted us for six weeks. Six weeks, Ray? We thought she was dead.

RAY: Why did she run off?

LEN: You tell me. I always provided a good home for her. She wanted for nothing. Two weeks before she was due to start Welsh Studies at Cardiff University, she disappeared.

RAY: Without a word?

LEN: Not a peep. I have another son. He's a lecturer in the local tech. He did everything we ever asked of him. But this girl? I don't know ... and to cap it all, she married an Englishman. It's like she's doing everything she can think of to defy me.

RAY: Do you have to take it so personal? Maybe she just wanted to live in London?

LEN: It's funny how, when it comes to my daughter, I'm only imagining things. You've just been rowing with your own family.

RAY: That's right. I have a daughter I hardly ever see.

LEN: Who was it said daughters always love their fathers?

RAY: My daughter Helen had Kate when she was 16. The father didn't want to know. Then she had two more children to two different men. Now she lives with a bastard who beats her. Poor Kate's always been torn between her mother and us.

LEN: But at least you still see your daughter.

RAY: Only to row.

LEN: At least you have that.

RAY: Well, get on the phone and you can row with yours.

LEN: I can't.

RAY: Why not?

LEN: I don't speak to her.

RAY: I thought you arranged to meet her?

LEN: I didn't arrange anything. My wife did it all.

RAY: Well, for heaven's sake, Len, lift the phone.

LEN: I'm her father. Why doesn't she ring me?

RAY: Len, the world knows your children are not your children. They came from us, but they don't belong to us. We can give them our love, but not our thoughts. All we are is bows, to be bent back as far as needed, so that the arrows can fly off. In their own direction.

[HUGO *enters, singing. He is wearing a party hat, streamers etc.*]

HUGO: 'When you're in love with a beautiful woman
   You watch your friends
   You watch your— '
RAY: Where have you been?
HUGO: Seeing your granddaughter safely to her car, where do you think?
RAY: You left half-an-hour ago.
HUGO: She was upset.
RAY: I bet you've been to a pub.
HUGO: No, I was down at the festival trying to score. But they only laughed at me. Then I went over to the group that was playing and asked them if they knew any flamingo music. But they were from the Dutch Ivory Coast or somewhere.
RAY: I haven't heard flamenco in years.
HUGO: I still do it in the Spanish Club on the first Friday of every month. Sex to music it is, what? Oh, and I was talking to Mrs. Bradford on the stairs.
RAY: What about?
HUGO: Nothing much. But she invited me in.
RAY: She did not.
HUGO: She did.
RAY: What for?
HUGO: I suppose the woman's lonely.
RAY: Rubbish.
HUGO: She is.
RAY: And what happened?
HUGO: I gave her one.
RAY: You what?
HUGO: You heard me.
RAY: That's a lie.
HUGO: Really, it was at her insistence.
RAY: You're an awful liar, Hugo.
HUGO: I don't know why I like women. They're one great big walking lie from head to toe, aren't they?
RAY: How do you make that out?
HUGO: Their appearance. What you see isn't what you get. Start with the hair. They dye it, bleach it, rinse it, perm it, curl it, even wear wigs. Then there's all that powder and paint on their faces, earrings, necklaces. Then you have shoulder pads, stuffed bras, push-up bras, girdles, tights, high heels. High heels, the biggest con of them all. What elegance a pair of high heels gives to the female

form. It's a bit like what the Eiffel Tower does for an ordinary city like Paris. Still, Mrs. Bradford does have a nice pair of legs.

RAY: Hugo, you have as much chance of pulling Mrs. Bradford as Fulham have of winning the European Cup.

HUGO: Who? She's mad about me. [*At this,* LEN, *who has been preoccupied, turns to the others. He has been crying.*]

LEN: I haven't seen my beautiful daughter in seven years. [*The others are silent, embarrassed.*] I've two little granddchildren, my own flesh and blood, I've never set eyes on. You know, you rear your children to the best of your ability. I had no idea how she felt. I really had no idea. She wrote a letter to her mother, saying how she hated me. How I gave her no childhood. I was always away, always out on trade union business, politics, never there when she needed me. I spent my life saving the workers and losing my own daughter. I have to get to Putney Bridge station. Is there a phone, Ray?

RAY: In the hall.

HUGO: Sit down. Sit down and have a last drink before you go.

LEN: I'll have to phone.

HUGO: Here, Len. Have a drink and we'll have a last yarn. Then we'll all go home. [HUGO *pours* LEN *and drink and sits him down.*] What about it, eh?

LEN: I've never drank so much in all my life.

HUGO: Since the day you walked up the middle of Gandesa in your underpants! And tried to kiss Josephina, the cook.

LEN: I did not.

HUGO: You did.

RAY [*preoccupied*]: How was Kate, Hugo?

HUGO: What?

RAY: When you took her to the car? What did she say?

HUGO: Well, she did mention something about going to buy an AK47 automatic assault rifle.

RAY: What did she say?

HUGO: She's annoyed, to put it mildly.

RAY: Tough.

HUGO [*pointing*]: You were OTT.

RAY: Who?

HUGO: I think your granddaughter is genuinely trying to help you. She told me about your Alzheimer's. You have to watch it, Ray.

RAY: Hold on a minute. A couple of hours ago, you two were on my side.

LEN: That's before we heard her side of the story.

RAY: What about mine?

HUGO: She's adamant, Ray. She told me to tell you, if you don't ring her within 24 hours, she's never coming back.

RAY: I will not be dictated to.

LEN: Heavens, you know, the older you get, the more your family problems accumulate.

HUGO: Speak for yourself. I have no offsprings. Except for the childer in Barcelona. But that's another story.

LEN: We three, we've a lot in common. We've given a hell of a lot of our lives to politics, to public life. I suppose something has to suffer.

HUGO: I worked at the building game all my life and I've lost count how many times I was shown my cards simply because I was a communist. I was a good spark, too. Wired the BBC Television Centre in six weeks.

LEN: Sometimes, you wonder why men do it?

HUGO: Well, when you're in a real political party, like me and Ray, you know why you do it. Right, Ray?

RAY: Maybe it's all just to do with ego.

HUGO: Ego?

RAY: The need to go into public life, to do good, to have our names mentioned, to be praised, to be loved. All ego.

HUGO: So I went to Spain and risked my shagging life just so somebody would say nice things about me?

RAY: No. But there may have been other reasons.

HUGO: Like what?

RAY: Personal reasons. Things we might have pushed to the back of our heads at the time.

HUGO: Well, I went to Spain to fight fascism. What did you go for?

[*The young men jump to their feet.*]

YOUNG LEN: The sun!

YOUNG HUGO: Women!

YOUNG RAY: The food!

YOUNG HUGO: Sex!

[*The young men dart forward, taking up covering positions in and around the old men.*]

YOUNG LEN [*suddenly itchy*]: And the dreaded lice! I now hate the lice more than I hate Franco. I propose that the war should be brought to a temporary halt so that both sides can come together to declare war on the lice.

YOUNG RAY: Give over, Bussell. We've just crossed the River Ebro on another offensive. Franco'll be finished in six months.

YOUNG LEN: Another six months of this? Bombs, bullets, trenches, starvation, unbearable heat during the day and freezing cold at night.

YOUNG RAY: Well, we all knew what we signed up for.

[*The young men change positions again.*]

YOUNG HUGO: Strange you should say that. When we were lying in reserve yesterday, Josephina's brother started talking to me.

YOUNG RAY: Edmondo?

YOUNG HUGO: He asked me what I was doing here. [*Laughter*]

YOUNG LEN: He what?

YOUNG RAY: Did you not tell him you're here to look for Lope de Vegas' 2,000 long-lost plays?

YOUNG LEN: What did you say?

YOUNG HUGO: I told him I was fighting Franco, and he said, 'Yes, but what else are you doing here?'

YOUNG RAY: Was Edmondo drunk?

YOUNG HUGO: I don't know, but he insisted there had to be another reason. He said there had to be a more personal reason.

YOUNG RAY: I'm guilty! I want to take it out on Franco for making me miss all Fulham's home games this season.

YOUNG LEN: Well, there's nothing personal in it for me. I came all the way from Blaengarw for one thing and one thing only. To defend the democratically-elected government of Spain.

YOUNG RAY: What did you tell Edmondo?

YOUNG HUGO: Nothing. But when he wasn't looking I pissed in his coffee.

[*More shelling. The men cover their heads.*]

YOUNG RAY: Len?

YOUNG LEN: Over here.

YOUNG RAY: Hugo! [*Silence*] Hugo! [*Longer silence*]

YOUNG HUGO: What?

YOUNG RAY: You bugger.

HUGO: That Edmondo. He used to do my head in, insisting we must have had other reasons for going to Spain. He was a right moonbeam.

RAY: I went to fight fascism. But, if I'm really honest, a lot of it had to do with Rachel Precott.

HUGO: Rachel Prescott?

RAY: Part of me actually went to Spain to try and make her jealous. To make her love me more.

HUGO: You can't be serious.

LEN: I was in absolutely no doubt about my eagerness to fight

Franco. But sometimes sitting in the warm Spanish sun made me realise how much I hated working down the pit. Going to Spain stopped me from dying of boredom. Unfortunately, it also drove my mother to an early grave. She took my going very badly. Then, when she heard I was in Burgos prison, she took a mild stroke.

YOUNG LEN: When I get home, I'm taking my mother on a full week's holiday to Colwyn Bay and I'll wait on her hand and foot.

LEN: Then she was told I'd been sentenced to death and executed. She refused to believe it and wrote letters to MPs and newspapers.

YOUNG LEN: She loves the cinema. I'll take her to the cinema every day.

LEN: I was in Burgos for two years. And 19 days before I was released my mother died.

RAY: When did you find out she had died?

LEN: I arrived off the train at Victoria Station to be met by a welcoming party of hundreds of people. MPs, friends, well-wishers, reporters. People were singing and clapping me on the back and my brother called me aside and told me ... my mother was dead. Two minutes later, I had to make a speech to the crowd.

RAY: That must have been dreadful, Len.

HUGO: The day I joined the Communist Party—the 8th January, 1935—my da stopped speaking to me. He used to pass me on the stairs in silence. He was a ferocious Catholic. A member of the Clonard Confraternity, which is kinda like ... being a priest but you're still allowed to have sex. He built an altar to Our Lady above my bed. The morning I left to go to Spain, my mother hugged me and cried. But my father pushed past me and hurried on to work.

YOUNG HUGO: I'm going back to Belfast, and I'm gonna walk into our house and tell my da to catch himself on.

HUGO: I walked into our house at exactly a quarter past eight on a Saturday morning and held my hand out for my da to shake it. This is after being away for two years. And he got up, put his coat on and walked past me out into the street.

YOUNG HUGO: Then I'm going on to become general secretary of the Communist Party of Ireland.

HUGO: Six months later, I had a major row with the party in Belfast and took off for London.

YOUNG RAY: I'm going to make a big pot of real English tea, buy a season ticket for Fulham, then I'm going to find a nice girl from the party to accompany me for walks over Clapham Common.

RAY: I made a beeline straight for Rachel's house, but she'd gone to

the Channel Islands to marry that solicitor of hers. I literally
didn't eat for three days. Because of my profile in Spain, I
couldn't get a job back in Fleet Street. That's when I hired my
first lorry and started buying and selling scrap metal.

YOUNG RAY: Well, in the meantime, folks, we've still got the Ebro in
front of us. Two days leave, then it's back out for the second half.
With the wind against us.

YOUNG HUGO: But we are a couple of goals up. We are in front.

YOUNG LEN: If only I were playing a leisurely game of football on
Blaengarw village green.

YOUNG RAY: I'd give up a week's smokes to be standing on the
terraces cheering on Fulham.

YOUNG HUGO: I'd give up a year's smokes to get into Josephina's
knickers.

YOUNG LEN: Your language is atrocious, Hugo.

YOUNG RAY: I'm going to tell Edmondo how you've been talking
about his skin and blister.

YOUNG HUGO: No, Ray, don't be doing that. What with me going out
with Josephina at the moment.

YOUNG RAY and **YOUNG LEN:** You what?

YOUNG HUGO: Josephina. Me and her's going kinda steady at the minute.

YOUNG RAY: You are mad, Hugo.

YOUNG LEN: Josephina's boyfriend is a political commissar at the
front and she never looks at other men.

YOUNG HUGO: Is that so?

YOUNG RAY: I've known her nearly a year now and I can't get her to smile.

YOUNG LEN: I wrote her a poem and she tore it up in front of my face.

YOUNG RAY: She has absolutely no interest in men.

YOUNG HUGO: That's strange, because I've been seeing her for six
weeks now. We've been to Madrid together, I've met her family in
Alcaniz. She's terrific in bed. You two are way behind the times.

YOUNG RAY: You're a liar.

YOUNG LEN: It's impossible.

YOUNG HUGO: Want me to prove it?

YOUNG RAY: Yeah.

YOUNG LEN: Yeah. Prove it.

YOUNG HUGO: Okay.

> [JOSEPHINA *enters.* YOUNG HUGO *smartens himself up. He looks across
> at* JOSEPHINA.]

YOUNG HUGO [*to others*]: You wouldn't do me a favour?

YOUNG RAY: What?

YOUNG HUGO: Well, because we are members of the same unit, she has insisted that we only meet secretly. If you would ... [*Beckons them away*]

YOUNG RAY: Oh yes, right.

YOUNG LEN: Yes, but how are you going to prove anything?

YOUNG HUGO [*hesitatingly*]: You'll ... a ... you'll see me kissing her.

YOUNG RAY: You're on.

[YOUNG RAY *and* YOUNG LEN *hide behind the outhouse door, ready to listen and look.* YOUNG HUGO *approaches* JOSEPHINA.]

YOUNG HUGO: Buenos dias, Josephina.

JOSEPHINA: Buenos dias.

YOUNG HUGO [*haltingly*]: A que hora sirven el almuerzo?

JOSEPHINA [*loudly*]: No entiendo, no entiendo!

YOUNG HUGO: Shushhh. Y'don't have to shout. Okay, since you've been getting lessons from the Americans, we'll try the English. [*Quietly, careful for the others not to hear*] Josephina ... why do you ignore me?

JOSEPHINA [*loudly*]: I don't ignore you.

YOUNG HUGO: Shushhh! I've asked you to go out with me, walk with me, talk with me, even let me help you cook, but ... but you stare at me as if I wasn't there. I love you, Josephina.

JOSEPHINA: You're nuts. There is a battle on, a fight on. Go and fight fascists.

YOUNG HUGO: You don't realise, Josephina, a word from you, a kind word from you, for me, would be like winning a village from the fascists.

JOSEPHINA: You're bananas.

YOUNG HUGO: A kiss from you would be like us retaking San Sebastian. Making love to you would be as beautiful as chasing Franco out of Spain.

JOSEPHINA: You Irishman, you crazy. [*She turns to go.*]

YOUNG HUGO: Espere un momento? [*She stops.*] I thought I should let you know tonight is the last meal you will be cooking for me.

JOSEPHINA: Good. You go home.

YOUNG HUGO: No.

[*Over behind the outhouse door*]

YOUNG LEN: What's he saying?

YOUNG RAY: I can't hear.

YOUNG LEN: He doesn't seem to be getting very far. [*They laugh.*]

YOUNG HUGO: No, I'm not going home. I'm going to die. I have been selected by the great General Lister to go on a special mission to kill Franco.

JOSEPHINA [*suddenly interested*]: You? General Lister?

YOUNG HUGO: Yes. He wanted one man to give up his life to get close enough to Franco to kill him and I have been selected. I will be dead in ... 24 hours.

JOSEPHINA: Ohhh.

YOUNG HUGO: But I will die proudly, for the freedom of Spain. When victory comes to democratic Spain, I know my sacrifice will not have been in vain.

[JOSEPHINA *is deeply moved and rushes to embrace and kiss* YOUNG HUGO. *The others are amazed.*]

YOUNG RAY: They're kissing.

YOUNG LEN: He was telling the truth.

YOUNG RAY: Lucky bugger.

YOUNG LEN: For once, he was telling the truth.

JOSEPHINA: Oh, poor Hugo.

YOUNG HUGO [*loudly*]: Will you do something for me, Josephina?

JOSEPHINA: I will do anything for you.

YOUNG HUGO [*loudly*]: Before we go to bed tonight, will you teach me to dance flamingo?

JOSEPHINA: I shall dance with you until the stars leave the sky. [*She kisses him and exits.*]

YOUNG RAY: You lucky bugger.

YOUNG LEN: How did you manage it?

YOUNG HUGO: Ach, she's just another woman. This oul' Spain is turning out not all that bad after all, is it? How long did you say, Ray, it would take us to defeat Franco?

YOUNG RAY: About six months.

YOUNG HUGO: Surely we could make it last a bit longer than that.

[HUGO *is sitting on a chair. He takes out a few marijuana cigarettes. He lights one up for himself and calls* LEN.]

HUGO: Here, Len. Have another one of these magic Woodbines. [LEN *comes across and kneels down in front of* HUGO, *who places a cigarette in his mouth and lights it.*] There you go. [LEN *inhales deeply, then lies down on the floor beside* HUGO. *At this,* JOSEPHINA *enters. She is carrying a bottle of wine and a glass. She approaches* YOUNG HUGO.]

JOSEPHINA: Hugo, Hugo, you must come. [*She hands him the glass and pours him some wine.*] My brother, Edmondo, and my other sisters. We have a party for you. You must come. [*She holds out her hand to* YOUNG HUGO. *The three men are stunned.*]

YOUNG HUGO: A party for me?

JOSEPHINA: This is your last night on this world and we want to make you happy. Please, you must come now.

[YOUNG HUGO *takes her hand and stands up. She leads him off, smiling at him.* YOUNG RAY *and* YOUNG LEN *look at each other, puzzled, then jump to their feet.*]

YOUNG RAY: Hey, wait for us!

YOUNG LEN: Don't start the party without us!

YOUNG RAY: Did you hear her say 'sisters'?

[*They rush off.* HUGO *is on the chair.* LEN, *flat on his back, is singing* 'The Deeply Dippy Song' *by Right Said Fred.* HUGO *is urging him on and joining in the chorus.*]

LEN [*singing*]: 'Oh my love, I can't make head nor tail of passion
Oh my love, let's sail on seas of passion now ... '

[*The song ends and both men laugh.*]

HUGO: You're full of surprises, Len. How the hell do you know that song? [*They both lift their cigarettes.*]

LEN: I babysit my little granddaughter and she plays it non-bloody-stop. She can sing it in Welsh, you know. The question is how do you know it?

HUGO: I never miss *Top of the Pops*. [*More laughter*]

LEN: God, these cigarettes are great.

HUGO: You like it?

LEN: I love it. God, if I'd been on these during my trade union days, there wouldn't have been any bloody strikes.

HUGO: That's how I discovered it. Remember the Wapping dispute? After two weeks on the picket line, a very nice *Sunday Times* journalist initiated me. After that, I couldn't get enough of it. Can you imagine what I looked like? A 72-year-old pensioner tramping in and out of the pubs in Hammersmith trying to score a ten-deal. After a while, I said 'Bugger this for a game of monopoly.' Now, I grow my own.

LEN: You do not!

HUGO: Bloody right I do. The wife waters it every day. She thinks it's an umbrella plant. [*At this, loud Spanish flamenco music is heard from the street.*]

HUGO: Ah! Flamingo!

LEN: Flamenco!

[HUGO *takes to the floor in flamenco pose. The music gets louder.* HUGO *dances. He is joined by* LEN. HUGO *doesn't fancy* LEN *for a partner.*]

HUGO: I think I'll get Mrs. Bradford.

LEN: Yeah.

RAY [*struggling up*]: Never mind Mrs. Bradford. I'll dance with you.
[*The three men dance at downstage right. Upstage, the three young men and* JOSEPHINA *enter with bottles of wine and a flurry of light and music.* JOSEPHINA *and* YOUNG HUGO *take centre stage and dance.* YOUNG RAY *is upstage and* YOUNG LEN *is downstage left. As* JOSEPHINA *continues to dance, the three old men link up with their three younger selves, the Rays upstage, the Hugos downstage and the Lens downstage right. As the music ends abruptly, the old men stare at their younger selves in a moment of recognition.*]

HUGO: I'm away to see Mrs. Bradford.
[HUGO *exits.* RAY *and* LEN *return to their seats.*]

JOSEPHINA: Now, I must go. Edmondo will be waiting. [*She kisses* YOUNG HUGO *quickly on the lips.*]

YOUNG HUGO: You can't go now.

JOSEPHINA: I must. Edmondo is waiting to drive me to Madrid. I have been elected a delagate to the party congress.

YOUNG HUGO: But what about me?

JOSEPHINA [*running off*]: Buenos noches!

YOUNG HUGO: I'll buenos noches you!
[YOUNG RAY *and* YOUNG HUGO *are drinking from bottles of wine.* YOUNG RAY *is very drunk.*]

YOUNG LEN: What do we do now?

YOUNG RAY: Let's go and get Franco!

YOUNG HUGO: I don't know about you, but I think I'll sneak off to Maria's house.

YOUNG LEN: Josephina's sister?

YOUNG HUGO: Yeah. When Josephina was on two days leave last week, I did it with her sister.

YOUNG LEN: Maria?

YOUNG HUGO: She's only 19. Loves it, she does.

YOUNG RAY: Right. Who wants to see a bottle of pissy Spanish vino disappearing right before your eyes?
[YOUNG RAY *puts the wine bottle to his mouth and makes a good attempt at finishing it in one go.*]

YOUNG LEN: Raymond Oliver. I've never seen you drunk before.

YOUNG RAY: That's because I've never been drunk before.

YOUNG LEN: That Spanish plonk is stronger than you think.

YOUNG HUGO: It's also my Spanish plonk. [*Snapping it back*]

YOUNG LEN: Too much of that stuff will do your heads in.

YOUNG RAY: At this very moment, there's more than wine doing my head in. Anybody fancy going home?

YOUNG LEN: And Rockerfella will give his money away to the downtrodden.

YOUNG RAY: I'm serious. I think it's time to go home.

YOUNG HUGO: Soda farls and a big plate of champ, with a big dab of margarine in the middle.

YOUNG RAY: The war's as good as over, lads. We're losing.

YOUNG LEN: No, it's not. Granted, it's not going our way at the moment. But I've a feeling things will turn our way very soon.

YOUNG HUGO: I got a new rifle yesterday.

YOUNG RAY: It's over. Are you blind? Hitler and Mussolini have stood by Franco, while we've been deserted by everyone except what little the Russians get through to us. The great fight for democratic Spain is over. [*Moving downstage*] Hugo, I want a share of your next girl or I'm placing you on a charge.

YOUNG HUGO: That's not fair.

[YOUNG RAY *lies down drunk.*]

YOUNG RAY: At least let me watch? [*He sleeps.*]

YOUNG LEN: When he gets into that state, there must be something wrong.

YOUNG HUGO: A month ago, we charged over the Ebro. Now, we're back on this side of the river. Franco's a bastard. Ray's right. Fascism is winning.

YOUNG LEN: I look forward to the day when Chamberlain and Roosevelt are staring up the nose of fascism.

YOUNG HUGO: When I left Belfast to come here, I can honestly say I had no idea it would be this bad. If it wasn't for him, I wouldn't be here.

YOUNG LEN: Same here. I arrived here the same day as a young fella called Charlie Donnelly from Tyrone. We were thrown straight into the battle at Jarama. On our first day, we were both deeply shocked by the ferocity of the fighting. We took an unmerciful pounding from Franco's artillery, hours before we even saw a fascist. Men were falling all over the place. A young English chap was hit and fell over me. His guts spilled out on to the ground. He says, 'I'm hit', and started to stuff his guts back into his belly with his hand. It was heart breaking. Soon, I found myself dug in below an olive tree with Charlie. The roar of guns all around us was unbearable. Every time a shell fell near me, my guts contracted and the blood sucked right out of my body. Above us, some olives had been burst and were dripping down on us. Charlie puts his hand up and squeezed a bunch. 'Look,' he said, 'even the olives are bleeding.' Two days later, our line broke and we retreated back to the sunken road. The men were shattered, demoralised, our commanders had been killed. Then Ray appeared from nowhere. He began to bark orders. He went over to one man, physically stood him up, dusted him down and put his rifle back in his hand. He went along the road cajoling, urging, pleading, until hundreds of men were stood up and ready to go back into the line. Ray and Jock Cunningham then marched at the head of us. Ray got someone to start singing 'The Internationale' and, before we knew it, we'd taken back our positions. Sounds corny, but that's exactly how it happened. I saw it with my own eyes.

YOUNG HUGO: After my first day at Brunete, I found myself lying in a shell hole, shivering and shocked out of my life. Ray came up, found a blanket, put it over me, told me everything would be alright. And it was.

YOUNG LEN: He's a natural leader of men.

YOUNG HUGO: He and Eamon Downey were a good combination.

YOUNG LEN: Eamon put it in words.

YOUNG HUGO: And Ray made it happen. It's hard to accept that Eamon is dead.

YOUNG LEN: Two days his body lay in no-man's-land. No one knowing if he was alive or dead. [YOUNG RAY, *lying prone on the ground, stirs.*] Well, what are we going to do about him?

YOUNG HUGO: There's only one thing for it. [*They lift* YOUNG RAY *up.*]

YOUNG LEN: What's that?

YOUNG HUGO: I'll have to get him a girl somewhere or I'm in big trouble. [*Moving off*] I could put a word in with Dolores from the field hospital. But she wants to marry me.

YOUNG RAY [*singing*]: 'Oh the shark has sharpened teeth now ... '
[*The others join in the singing as they exit. Ray's living room.* RAY *and* LEN *are in earnest discussion.*]

RAY: Hugo's been a good friend to me. I mean it. A good friend.

LEN: Yes, and all the more reason why he should know about your decision.

RAY: What good would it do? I'm 81 and I probably don't have long to live.

LEN: You have to be true to yourself.

RAY: Hugo's always been so straight with me.

LEN: But he never told you how Eamon Downey died.

RAY: I don't know what you mean.

LEN: Hugo was there. He was there when Eamon died.

RAY: No, he wasn't.

LEN: Ray. Hugo was there. I know. After I was released from Burgos,

I met a man from Liverpool. He told me he ended up in the next
hospital bed to Hugo after the battle of Brunete. He said Hugo
was in a terrible state and told him everything that happened.
[YOUNG HUGO *hurries on, agitated, stands in a spot.*]

YOUNG HUGO: I was beside Eamon. Not right beside him, but close.
When we got the orders, we charged forward, but they were
waiting. Jesus Christ, it was open slaughter. Men fell all around
me. There was nothing we could do but turn back. I saw Eamon
falling. He shouted, 'I'm hit! I'm hit!' The rest of us just ran like
hell. It was every man for himself. When we got back to our
lines, I realised I was wounded in the leg. It was a small flesh
wound. Then I heard Eamon. He started calling my name again.
He pleaded. I didn't know what to do. The fascists had us
pinned down. I couldn't do anything. We listened to Eamon
moaning all night, right through the night. Death sounds. It was
awful, bloody awful. Jesus Christ, it was awful ...

RAY: Hugo never told me that.

LEN: So you don't owe Hugo anything.

RAY: What are you saying? Are you trying to say he did something wrong?

LEN: I'm merely pointing out that all this allegiance you have to Hugo
... it wasn't always returned. He wasn't always straight with you.

[*Door opens and* HUGO *enters, solemn-faced. He stops beside* YOUNG HUGO.]

HUGO: I have a confession to make. [*Silence*] I never got an erection
the whole time I was in Spain.

LEN: You what?

HUGO: A hardner. I never got one in two years. The stresses of war.

LEN: What about all the women? Didn't you sleep with Josephina?

HUGO: That's another confession. I didn't. She fancied you.

LEN: Me?

HUGO: I never got within a snooker cue of her.

LEN: So why didn't she approach me?

HUGO: 'Cause I told her you had VD. [YOUNG HUGO *rushes off.*]

LEN: You dirty ... [*The men laugh.* HUGO *pours some drinks*] How did
you get on with Mrs. Bradford?

HUGO: Fine. We had a drink. Now she's dancing with a wee
Pakistani man. Here, she was talking about you, Ray. She said
you two get together regularly for wee drinks. I think you two are
a number, Ray? What's the story?

RAY: I think you need psychiatric help.

LEN: I would agree there.

HUGO: Here, and she told me a smasher, Ray. She said you and her got drunk together the night the Berlin Wall came down. Now, is that true or is it not true?

LEN: I think he did.

HUGO: She says, she says you helped her to write a letter to that bastard Gorbachev thanking him for letting the wall come down. That's when I realised she was definitely off her trolley. [HUGO *roars laughing.*]

LEN: I watched the Berlin Wall coming down with my wife and we both got so excited we cried. It was the most wonderful occasion.

HUGO: It was betrayal.

LEN: For heaven's sake, Hugo, are you never going to change?

HUGO: Am I going to betray the working-class? No. Never.

LEN: You can't continue with exactly the same set of politics after such monumental changes have taken place. You can't be thinking straight.

HUGO: In your book, if a man sticks to the same basic principles that first inspired him, he's not thinking straight. In my book, it's called guts. Having the bottle to stick by your beliefs, even when they become unpopular.

LEN: Hugo. Stalinism was wrong in the 1930s and it's even more wrong in the 1990s. Thank God Mikhail Gorbachev came along.

HUGO: Typical Labour Party twaddle. 'Communism's wrong. Capitalism's flawed, but we think we can make it work.' Capitalism is immoral and evil and I'll never stop believing that.

LEN: I agree.

HUGO: You don't. You only pretend to agree. You accept capitalism.

LEN: Until we have something better in its place.

HUGO: So, in the meantime, we live with poverty and exploitation?

LEN: Whatever. But we can't have any more Berlin Walls.

HUGO: Ray? Ray, do you hear this tripe?

RAY: I hear it.

HUGO: Tell Mr. Half-a-Loaf, here, what we fought for. Tell him what we went to Spain for.

LEN: Hugo, I went to Spain, too.

HUGO: What for? A sun tan?

LEN: For very similar reasons to you. But I didn't go to bring Stalinism to Spain.

HUGO: Ray, will you talk to this man? He seems to forget the great achievements of communism this century. Remind him that the best men and women in every country in the world, the best brains, the greatest workers, the noblest hearts, gave their all to communism. It has been the most unselfish, pure-hearted, political movement in the history of man. Tell him that, Ray.

RAY: Everything you've said about communism is perfectly true. But ... [*Pause*] ... it's dead.

[HUGO *stares at* RAY *for a long time. Silence.* HUGO *shifts.*]

HUGO: What do you mean, it's dead?

RAY: I mean, it was a great dream. It was tried and it's dead. [*Holding his hands up*] Manos arriba. End of story.

HUGO: Are you alright? Are you sure you know what you're saying? [RAY *nods firmly.*] Ray. This is the Alzheimer's talking. You're not a bit well.

RAY: There isn't a thing wrong with me.

HUGO: But, Ray. Things are beginning to turn around again. It's on the upsurge in Poland, there's signs in Russia, Cuba's remained firm. Ray, we have to hold on.

RAY: Hugo, the Cup Final's over. We were trounced. We lost.

HUGO: That's what you think, what you really think?

RAY: It's how it is.

HUGO: I pushed your wheelchair on to a platform a year ago for you to receive a long-service award from the general secretary of the party.

RAY: And like the coward that I've been, I let you do it.

HUGO: You made a fool out of me.

RAY: I made a fool out of myself.

LEN: The world's changing, Hugo. We all have to change with it. That's what Gorbachev recognised.

HUGO: No. It's the other way round. As Marx said, the point is we have to change the world.

RAY: Every time I saw Gorbachev on the TV, he brought me joy. He brought sheer joy into this battered old heart.

HUGO: He betrayed his own party.

RAY: He had to betray his party to be true to the growth and freedom of his people.

HUGO [*standing up*]: I've heard enough. You might have thrown the towel in, Ray, but I haven't. Nobody can ever tell me this world still isn't made up of the haves and the have-nots. And I know which side I'm on. [HUGO *is preparing to leave.*]

RAY: Sit down, Hugo.

HUGO: And listen to this guff?

LEN: Surely we can agree to disagree?

RAY: C'mon, Hugo. Sit down and have another drink.

HUGO [*angrily*]: Stuff the drink.

LEN: Take it easy, Hugo.

HUGO: This is a great blow, Ray. I came here hoping to get some inspiration from you, some common sense. Just like in the old days, in Spain. You always knew exactly what to say, what to do. Like the morning you read us Eamon Downey's poem. That morning changed me. I vowed to fight for communism till the day I died. I believed in you. You used to inspire me, Ray. I always looked up to you ... now, now you're ... you're no more than a rat. A dirty, stinking, spineless rat. You're a treacherous bastard. Eamon Downey will be turning in his grave. He gave his life in Spain for what? For you to do this? Eamon Downey's arse is a better man than you! [*Exits*]

RAY: That's why I didn't want to do it. I didn't want to lose Hugo, and all the others. I didn't want to let go.

LEN: I'll pour you a drink.

RAY: Please.

LEN: It's nearly midnight, Ray. Maybe I'd better stay here tonight. Can I sleep on your sofa?

RAY: Only if you don't snore.

[*The men chuckle. Drinks are poured.* RAY *knocks back his drink in one.*]

LEN: Don't worry, Ray. I'm sure you did the right thing.

RAY: There is no future. We're living at the end of hope. When we were young, we could dream great dreams. Now, what have the kids got? Materialism and nationalism. Bosnia. Northern Ireland. We have to sit back and watch narrow-minded men fight over lines on the map. Nationalism is scrumpy compared to the vintage bottle of wine that socialism was. All those wasted years.

LEN: Stop talking humbug, man.

RAY: I've wasted my whole life. Even my body is failing me.

LEN: Maybe it's telling you to shut up.

RAY: Even Fulham never did much. I have to ring Kate.

[*As* RAY *shuffles to stage right,* JOSEPHINA *emerges on a raised platform.*]

JOSEPHINA: I, Josephina Caricedo Martinez, as executive member of the party congress, am very proud to make this address. It is very hard to say a few words in farewell to the heroes of the International Brigades. A feeling of sorrow, an infinite grief, catches our throats. Mothers! Women of Spain! When the years pass by and the wounds of war are being staunched, then speak to your children. Tell them of the these men of the International Brigades.

YOUNG LEN [*enters*]: Kit Conway, Tipperary, Ireland.

JOSEPHINA: Tell them how they gave up everything ...

YOUNG LEN: John Cornford, Oxford.

JOSEPHINA: ... their youth, their loves, their countries, their families, and came to us ...

YOUNG HUGO [*enters*]**:** William Meredith, Cardiff.

JOSEPHINA: Today, they are going away. Many of them, thousands of them, are staying here with the Spanish earth for their shroud ...

YOUNG LEN: Alec McDade, Glasgow.

JOSEPHINA: Comrades of the International Brigades, you can go proudly ...

YOUNG HUGO: Charlie Donnelly, Tyrone, Northern Ireland.

JOSEPHINA: You are history. You are legend ...

YOUNG RAY [*enters*]**:** Wally Tapsell, London.

JOSEPHINA: We shall not forget you ...

YOUNG RAY: Ralph Cantor, Manchester.

JOSEPHINA: And when the olive tree of peace puts forth its leaves again, entwined with the laurels of the Spanish Republic's victory, come back!

YOUNG LEN: William Tumilson, Belfast.

JOSEPHINA: Long live the heroes of the International Brigades!

YOUNG HUGO: Willie Keegan, Glasgow.

YOUNG LEN: Johnny Stevens, Leeds.

YOUNG HUGO: Eamon McGrotty, Derry.

YOUNG RAY: Tommy Patton, Achill Island. Eamon Downey, Belfast.

[KATE *enters the flat with suitcase and Ray's coat. We hear Caribbean music.*]

KATE: I see the community festival is still going strong. Do you want me to shut the window?

RAY: No, they're alright. Thanks for coming back. [*Pause*] Manos arriba.

KATE: You pushed me to the wire.

RAY: I know. I almost added you to my list of casualties.

KATE: I forgive you.

RAY: You've been right about most things.

KATE: Hurry up and put your coat on. Oh, I found this in your wardrobe. [*Holds up his Spanish Civil War hat.*] Do you want to take it with you?

RAY: I'll do better than that. I'll bloody well wear it. [*He puts the hat on.*] It's been one hell of game.

KATE: There's still a lot to play for.

RAY: Yes. And, if I close my eyes, I can still paint a few pictures.

KATE: You look good. They'll love you.

RAY: I feel good. In the humble words of the poet, 'I feel like the green shoot, waiting for the flower'.

Black-out

RINTY

Rinty was first performed at the Group Theatre, Belfast, August 1990. The set was designed by James Helps. The director was Ian Rickson. The cast was as follows:

Young Rinty   Michael Liebmann
Old Rinty   Joe McPartland

All the other minor characters were played by Gerry McGrath and Catherine Brennan. They are:

Choke-the-Dog
Oul' James
Bunty Doran
Theresa
Charlie Tosh
Sarah
Frances
Martha Monaghan
Frank McAlornan
Maxie etc

ACT ONE

Dark stage. A boxing ring dominates the stage and becomes the playing areas for most of the action. Fade-up to dim light shining from a street gas lamp. We hear noises and voices off.

CHOKE-THE-DOG [*loud and raucous*]: Go and ballicks yourself! A married your daughter, not you! Nigh frig off back to your own house, y'oul' ...
[*Fade-up girls singing*]

GIRLS: 'In and out goes Dusty Bluebells
In and out goes Dusty Bluebells
In and out goes Dusty Bluebells ... '
[*Fade-up girls singing and fade-up men singing*]

MAN: 'Craigavon sent the Specials out
To shoot the people down
He thought the IRA was dead
In dear old Belfast town ... '
[*Fade-down singing. We hear the horn of the Liverpool boat on its way up the lough. A sick man coughs loudly, repeatedly.*]

BARNEY [*shouting*]: Rayyyyyyyyy-eggs! Any oul' regs!

KAY [*shouting*]: Peter and Bobby! Yiz are awantin'—your dinner's poured out!

PADDY [*shouting*]: Best atin' apples nigh—four for tuppence, best a value, 'mon ahead, ladies!
[*We hear the sound of a horse-and-cart on cobblestones, factory horns etc.*]

BUBBLY DAN: Up the rebels! Up the Irish Republican Army!

MAISIE [*shouting*]: Go on, y'fenian bastard, and shout that outside your own door!
[*Fade-down young girls singing*]

GIRLS: 'On the hillside stands a lady

Who she is I do not know
All she wants is gold and silver ... '
[*Fade-up girls singing and fade-up man singing.*]

MAN: 'For we'll get a penny rope
And we'll hang the fuckin' Pope
On the 12th of July in the morning.'
[*Fade-down singing. Ship's horn again. The man coughing again.*]

GUESS METER [*drunk singing*]: 'Whennna firrrrst, I saw the
lovelight ... in your eyeeeeesa ...
I knewwa ... the world held not ...
but joy for meeeee ... '
[*Fade-down singinf and hold.* OLD RINTY *enters. He is smoking. He walks
casually to centre stage. He listens, cocking to hear a distant shout.*]

JIMMY [*shouting*]: Mrs. Munegin, Mrs. Munegin! Your Rinty's barred
from Peter's Hill Baths.

MRS. MONAGHAN: What for?

JIMMY: Instead of divin' off the dial, he dived off the roof!

MRS. MONAGHAN: It wouldn't be our John.

OUL' JOHN [*fading*]: Herrins! Fresh Ardglass herrins!

OLD RINTY: They say that no matter what y'do or where y'go
throughout your life—your first 15 years never leave ya.

This is where I grew up—a stone's throw from the Docks that
way, and a brisk walk to the top of the Cavehill that way.
[*Pointing*] Surrounded by linen mills and factories of every
description, our wee streets were crammed full with the biggest
collection of characters y'ever saw in your life.

These sounds, sights and smells never left me.

Not for one minute.

The year the Great War ended—1918—I was born over there
in number 23 Lancaster Street. I was christened John Joseph
Monaghan but later on, a took a likin' to a film, and because I
was the fastest boy in the district, m'granny called me after the
star of the film—*Rin-Tin-Tin*. This was soon shortened and the
name stuck—Rinty. Rinty Monaghan—the cheekiest wee bugger
in the district.

WEE MARY [*crying loudly*]: Mr. Munegin! Mr. Munegin!

MR. MONAGHAN: What ails ye, daughter?

WEE MARY: It's your Rinty.

MR. MONAGHAN: What about him?

WEE MARY: He bate me up.

MR. MONAGHAN: What for?

WEE MARY: 'Cos I wouldn't let him drown my cat.

MR. MONAGHAN: I'm goin' to kill that wee lad.

[MR MONAGHAN *exits.* CHOKE-THE DOG *enters. He speaks with a lisp.*]

CHOKE-THE-DOG: What's that y'have, Rinty?

[YOUNG RINTY *has been fiddling with something in his pocket.*]

YOUNG RINTY: What?

CHOKE-THE-DOG: That, in your hand.

YOUNG RINTY: Nothin'.

CHOKE-THE-DOG: It's not nothin'. I saw it. It's sumpin'.

YOUNG RINTY: Mind your own business, Choke-the-dog.

CHOKE-THE-DOG [*curious*]**:** Is it poison?

YOUNG RINTY: Nah.

CHOKE-THE-DOG [*shouting*]**:** Bullets! [*Gets excited, pointing accusingly*] That's bullets! 'Cause your da used d'be in the Free State Army!

YOUNG RINTY [*angrily*]**:** It's not!

CHOKE-THE-DOG: What is it then?

YOUNG RINTY [*pause, quietly*]**:** Snuff.

CHOKE-THE-DOG: Snuff?

YOUNG RINTY: Aye. M'granny's snuff. I go for it every day.

CHOKE-THE-DOG: What are y'gonna do with it?

YOUNG RINTY [*devilish smile*]**:** Take some. [YOUNG RINTY *opens the tin.*]

CHOKE-THE-DOG: Yucck!

YOUNG RINTY: Want some?

[YOUNG RINTY *holds out a pinch of snuff.* CHOKE-THE-DOG *jumps back.*]

CHOKE-THE-DOG: Get away. You're mad, Rinty. I'm gonna tell your da on you.

[YOUNG RINTY *turns sharply and glares at him, gritting his teeth.* YOUNG RINTY *looks at the pinch of snuff. He holds it to his nose watched avidly by* CHOKE-THE-DOG.]

CHOKE-THE-DOG: What does it do for ye anyway?

YOUNG RINTY: I don't know. Nailer says it gives women big ...

[YOUNG RINTY *holds his two hands out from his chest. The two boys look at each other and laugh.*]

CHOKE-THE-DOG: I heard it makes women have babies.

YOUNG RINTY: Well my granda takes it and he hasn't had no baby yet! D'ya want me d'tell ya what it really does for ya? [CHOKE-THE-DOG *nods.*] Gives ya brains.

CHOKE-THE-DOG: Bollicks!

YOUNG RINTY: Brains! Our teacher takes it and he's smart, so I'm gonna take it. [*Puts the snuff to nose*]

CHOKE-THE-DOG: I don't need it.

YOUNG RINTY: Hyre do you not need it?

CHOKE-THE-DOG: I'm on long division nigh. And a'm a good speller.

YOUNG RINTY: Spell sumpin'.

CHOKE-THE-DOG: Like what?

YOUNG RINTY: Dick.

CHOKE-THE-DOG: You're bein dirty.

YOUNG RINTY: A'm not. A mean Dick out of Dick and Dora.

CHOKE-THE-DOG: Oh.

YOUNG RINTY: Can y'spell it?

[CHOKE-THE-DOG *is deeply perplexed. He looks around him and bites his lip.*]

CHOKE-THE-DOG: What does it begin with?

YOUNG RINTY: You're a dunce, Choke-the-dog.

CHOKE-THE-DOG: Well, if you're so smart, you spell it?

[YOUNG RINTY *hesitates.*]

YOUNG RINTY: I don't have d'spell it—I know it. [*Changing the subject*] Right, Choke-the-dog, do y'want some brains or what?

CHOKE-THE-DOG: A don't know, Rinty. M'ma wants me d'become a solicitor, so I don't know if I need brains or what? What are you gonna be when y'grow up?

YOUNG RINTY: Don't know. Sumpin' good.

CHOKE-THE-DOG: A fireman?

YOUNG RINTY: Nah.

CHOKE-THE-DOG: A train-driver?

YOUNG RINTY: Nah.

CHOKE-THE-DOG: What then?

YOUNG RINTY: Sumpin' different ... Just sumpin' different.

[*Presently, Rinty's older sister runs on-stage with a yardbrush and a bucket of water.*]

SARAH: Rinty! Rinty! You're awantin'.

YOUNG RINTY: What for?

SARAH: M'mammy says it's your turn to help me wash up the yard.

YOUNG RINTY: Nah it's not!

SARAH [*aggressively*]: Whadid you say there?

YOUNG RINTY [*meekly*]: A'm comin'. See ya, Choke-the-dog.

CHOKE-THE-DOG: See ya, Rinty.

[OLD RINTY *enters. He hands* YOUNG RINTY *a yardbrush and wanders over to stand at stage left.*]

OLD RINTY: Me and our Sarah. [SARAH *throws the bucket over the yard. She and* YOUNG RINTY *start brushing.*] Sarah was the oldest in our house. I was next. A was always cheekin' her up.

SARAH: You clean out Bubbles' corner, he's your dog.

YOUNG RINTY: Frig off!

SARAH: What?

YOUNG RINTY: You clean it.

[SARAH *stops what she is doing, straightens up, looks over at* YOUNG RINTY, *absolutely livid. She marches across amd smacks* YOUNG RINTY *across the face. He falls down, crying.*]

SARAH: You do what I tell ye!

YOUNG RINTY [*crying*]: I'm gonna tell m'ma on you!

SARAH: If m'mammy was here she'd kill you. Nigh, start brushin'!

[SARAH *physically lifts* YOUNG RINTY *and makes him brush.* YOUNG RINTY *momentarily fights back but* SARAH *wins.*]

OLD RINTY: Our Sarah could handle me better than Jackie Paterson and Dado Marino put d'gether.

[YOUNG RINTY *brushes, sobbing.*]

SARAH: I'll teach ya d'cheek me up.

[*She looks across at him, beginning to regret her harshness. Pause.*]

SARAH: Aren't you supposed d'be singin' the night?

YOUNG RINTY [*snapping*]: No!

SARAH: Well, see if I care.

OLD RINTY: Even as a 12 year old I did a bit a singin' at the odd concert. 'Rinty Monaghan, the Singing Schoolboy', the called me—and our Sarah used d'teach me the words of the songs.

SARAH: You're d'be at St. Mary's Hall for seven a'clock t'night.

YOUNG RINTY: So.

SARAH: So? Y'don't even know the words of the song.

YOUNG RINTY: So.

SARAH: S'okay with me.

[SARAH *begins to brush. She occasionally glances over at* YOUNG RINTY *until she decides the moment is right to sing.*]

SARAH: 'I'm confessin' that I love you
Tell me do you really love me too ... '

[YOUNG RINTY *sneaks in a glance at Sarah.*]

'I'm confessin' that I need you
Honest I do, I need you every moment ... '

[SARAH *looks across at Young Rinty but he still appears to be in a foul mood.*]

SARAH: 'In your eyes I read such strange things ... '

[YOUNG RINTY *repeats after her.*]

YOUNG RINTY [*quietly*]: 'In your eyes I read such strange things ... '

[SARAH *smiles.*]

SARAH: 'But your lips deny they're true ... '

YOUNG RINTY [*bit louder*]: 'But your lips deny they're true ... '

SARAH: 'Will your answer really change things ... '
YOUNG RINTY [*normal*]: 'Will your answer really change things ... '
SARAH: 'Leaving me blue ... '
YOUNG RINTY: 'Leaving me blue ... '
      [SARAH *and* YOUNG RINTY *sing the last verse together in close harmony.*]
YOUNG RINTY and SARAH: 'I'm afraid someday you'll leave me
      Sayin' can we just be friends
      If you go you know you'll grieve me ... '
      [*Young Rinty's* DA *enters*]
DA: What the hell's all this racket about? [SARAH *and* YOUNG RINTY *fall
      silent.*] Yid think I reared a pile of canaries instead of childer.
OLD RINTY: M'da, Ta Monaghan was the seventh son of a seventh
      son. A tough oul' character. A seaman most of his life—at home
      he was a strict disciplinarian—a spit and polish man. Y'weren't
      allowed d'lie in bed when my oul' fella was home. 'Adison says
      four hours sleep is enough for anybody,' he used d'shout. He
      wouldn't even let ya out on the street unless your shoes were
      shinin' like Donaghadee lighthouse.
SARAH: Rinty's d'sing at the concert d'night and we were just rehearsin'.
DA: Singin's not all you're doin', hey boy, is it?
      [*He walks across and punches* YOUNG RINTY *in the stomach.* YOUNG
      RINTY *clutches his stomach, bending forward.*]
OLD RINTY: If he thought y'needed it, oul' Ta Monaghan wasn't
      adverse to givin' his sons a thump.
YOUNG RINTY: What was that for, da?
DA: You've been hingin' around the Labour Hall, I hear?
YOUNG RINTY: A man asked me d'sing in between the fights da,
      that's all.
DA: Is that right? Well, I know somebody who saw y'countin' your
      purse money on Saturday night.
      [YOUNG RINTY *glares across at* SARAH. *She looks the other way.*]
OLD RINTY: Sarah had caught me on in the shop orderin' three
      shillins worth a carmels, 25 bars of chocolate and 12 lollipops—
      all for m'self.
DA: Sarah, your ma wants ye. [SARAH *scampers off.*] What's all this
      about then?
YOUNG RINTY: It just happened, da. I was knockin' about outside the
      Labour Hall and a had a row with Pimple McKee. The man saw
      us fightin' and asked us did we want t'do it in the ring and get
      money. After three rounds all the men cheered and everything,
      and threw money into the ring.

DA: Did ya win?

YOUNG RINTY: The referee called it a draw.

DA: And it only happened the once? [YOUNG RINTY *shakes his head.*] No?

YOUNG RINTY: A've fought Pimple six times nigh.

DA: Six times! This is gettin' serious. [*Pause*] Are y'any good?

YOUNG RINTY: The man that runs the Labour Hall says a've got a good right hand.

DA: Did he?

YOUNG RINTY: A bled Pimple's lip in the last fight.

DA: Is that so? So y'definitely wanna be a boxer?

YOUNG RINTY: Yiss, da.

> [DA *again punches* YOUNG RINTY *in the stomach.* DA *lights up a cigarette. He turns a few things over in his mind.*]

DA: Right. 'Mon with me.

> [DA *and* YOUNG RINTY *walk across stage.*]

OLD RINTY: M'da had been a navy boxin' champion himself and he knew the game well. W'walked up Lancaster Street, up Thomas Street and half-way up Great Georges Street, he stopped and said d'me—

DA [*stops*]: Rinty, boxin's a tough, stinkin' game. But if that's what y'wanna do, y'must be dedicated?

OLD RINTY: I nodded. Says he—

DA: A'm takin' y'in here d'see a man that knows a boxer by the way he walks.

OLD RINTY: The man a met that night was oul' James McAloran and the place was McAloran's Gym.

> [*McAloran's Gym.* YOUNG RINTY, *in training gear, is briskly going through a number of physical exercises. Sitting cross-legged on a stool is* OUL' JAMES MCALORAN, *watching attentively. He wears a flat cap and a cigarette end is permanently hanging from his mouth. Occasionally, he looks at a stopwatch. Standing beside him, wearing a suit, is* FRANK MCALORAN, *also carefully observing* YOUNG RINTY.]

JAMES [*barking*]: Alright, the light beg! [YOUNG RINTY *immediately turns and starts punching at the light bag.*] The heavy beg! [YOUNG RINTY *switches to the heavy bag.*] The ball! [YOUNG RINTY *switches to the ball.* OLD RINTY *enters and observes.* FRANK MCALORAN *takes off his coat, rolls up his sleeves, places pads on his hands and enters the ring.*] The ring! Inda the ring! [YOUNG RINTY *jumps into the ring and begins punching at the pads on Frank's hands.*] C'mon, work, work, work! [*Pause*] Okay, that's it. That'll do ye! [YOUNG RINTY *leans on the ropes exhausted while* FRANK *speaks to him.*]

OLD RINTY: At the end of that first night in McAloran's Gym I wasn't fit d'tie m'shoe laces. A needed a wash, but McAloran's Gym wasn't the Grand Central Hotel—as I quickly found out.

YOUNG RINTY: God, I'm luckin' forward d'a shire. [*The two McAlorans stop and look at* YOUNG RINTY.] A shire? Know like water, freshen up?

JAMES: Y'can do what everybody else does.

YOUNG RINTY: What's that?

[JAMES *drops a bucket beside* YOUNG RINTY.]

JAMES: Go next door d'Mrs. McWilliams and get a bucket a water and throw it round yourself.

YOUNG RINTY: Cold water?

JAMES: Where d'ya think this is, Buckingham Palace?

[YOUNG RINTY *lifts the bucket and exits.*]

OLD RINTY: This was the famous McAloran's Gym—home of champions?—I was throwing buckets a cold water round me— remember in the winter it was ice-cold water—up until the day a retired as Champion of the World. Sometimes y'didn't have to.

JAMES: The roof's leakin' again, Frank.

FRANK: Good. The boxers can shire under it.

OLD RINTY: The floor was busted all over the place.

JAMES: Boxer Hall went through the floor last night.

FRANK: Whadaya want me d'do?

OLD RINTY: When the got round d'it, the floor was repaired with tea-chest lids. The McAlorans didn't give a shite what state the Gym was in. What the were good at was boxin'. Frank knew the game inside out but it was oul' James was the brains. A master technician. And he didn't like d'waste his time.

FRANK: What's wrong a haven't seen that young lad, McNulty, back?

JAMES: I toul him not d'come back.

FRANK: What for?

JAMES: It wasn't there. A've toul ye before, Frank, if a young fella doesn't shape up in a fortnight, he'll never shape up.

OLD RINTY: My fortnight was up.

[YOUNG RINTY *enters, ready for a night's training.*]

JAMES: Young Munegin? [YOUNG RINTY *approaches him, apprehensive.*]

YOUNG RINTY: Yiss, Mr. McAloran.

JAMES: Y'interested in the fight game?

OLD RINTY: Was I interested? I was in love with it.

YOUNG RINTY: I aa ...

JAMES: There's a fight for ye next week.

OLD RINTY: Yipee!

YOUNG RINTY: Thanks ...

OLD RINTY: How much am a gettin'?

YOUNG RINTY: Who am a fightin'?

JAMES: Hyre the hell do I know—but you're on five shillin's.

OLD RINTY: Five bob? I was gettin' more than that from nobbins at the Labour Hall.

YOUNG RINTY: Oh thanks Mr. McAloran, that's great, thanks.

[YOUNG RINTY *turns to go.*]

JAMES: And here? He's your manager.

[FRANK *comes over.* JAMES *exits.*]

FRANK: Only if y'want me, Rinty.

YOUNG RINTY: Certainly, Frank.

FRANK: 25 per cent?

YOUNG RINTY: No problem. [*They shake hands.* YOUNG RINTY *bursts into song.*] 'I'm sitten on top, top of the world
just rollen' along, just singin' a song
I'm chasin' the blues from above ... '

FRANK: We ... [*shouting*] We think y'can do well. James thinks you've got a good right hand.

YOUNG RINTY: Is that right?

FRANK: There's only one problem.

YOUNG RINTY: What's that?

FRANK: This singin' business?

YOUNG RINTY: Ach, it's just the odd concert, a bit a crack—y'know, y'like a wee bit a fun.

FRANK: Well, I hear y'sing all over the place—the Empire last night, the Opera House for three weeks. Yiv even been tap dancin'.

YOUNG RINTY: Sure it helps with the futwork! [RINTY *laughs.*]

FRANK: Well, a'm givin' ya forewarnin'. It's either one or the other.

[YOUNG RINTY *gives this some thought.*]

OLD RINTY: I loved singin'... but m'heart was set on the boxin'.

YOUNG RINTY: Okay, Frank—the singin's out.

FRANK: Good. Your next fight's at the Chapel Fields. Y'ever hear of Ma Copley?

YOUNG RINTY: A'm fightin' a woman?

FRANK: No. She's the promoter.

[MA COPLEY *enters, a stern, matronly, middle-aged woman.* YOUNG RINTY *gets stripped.*]

MA COPLEY: Your lad ready, Frank?

FRANK: Ready and waitin'.

MA COPLEY: Would y'take a change of opponent?

FRANK: Who is it?

MA COPLEY: The other lad's pulled out. A have a fella ready, but he's a stone heavier than this lad? Do y'still want the fight?

FRANK: A stone heavier?

MA COPLEY: That's all a can do.

FRANK: It's up d'you, Rinty?

YOUNG RINTY [*smiles broadly*]: Yeah sure, I'll take it.

[YOUNG RINTY *steps into the ring.* FRANK, MA COPLEY *and* OLD RINTY *step in with him and stand around him. They all become boxers.*]

OLD RINTY: M'first opponent was Sam Ramsey. [YOUNG RINTY *and* OLD RINTY *punch each other to the body furiously for several seconds.*] Fought a draw. [YOUNG RINTY *turns to* MA COPLEY.] Next was Jim Pedlow. [YOUNG RINTY *throws several punches at* MA COPLEY.] For three years a was undefeated, then at the beginning of 1937... [FRANK *staggers* YOUNG RINTY *with several punches.*] A lost d'Jim Keery from Lisburn. After that a tuck on all-comers and bate all-comers.

[YOUNG RINTY *rotates knock-out after knock-out with* FRANK, MA COPLEY *and* OLD RINTY.]

Then came July 1938 at the Oval football ground. My opponent was a young Scots lad—only 18 and fightin' his third fight—but his name was to live with me for the rest of m'life—Jackie Paterson. I was so confident. Thirty-one wins behind me. I thought this kid would be a doddle. In the 5th round I even started clowning and makin' faces at the crowd when—*Bang.* [YOUNG RINTY *gets KO'd.*] That was the first and last time I was ever knocked out. I said to myself afterwards—

YOUNG RINTY: What was that guy's name? Paterson? Jackie Paterson. Must remember that—

OLD RINTY: But there was another name I had to contend with—she'd a big knockout punch as well. A wee red-haired girl by the name of Frances Thompson. My da used to run bus excursions—that's when I first met her.

[YOUNG RINTY *is standing up on a moving bus. Two women are sitting in front of him.*]

THERESA: There's yer man, whadaya call him?

FRANCES: Who?

THERESA: Yer man, Rinty Monaghan,

FRANCES: What happened his face?

THERESA: He's a boxer. He's a lovely fella, Frances.

FRANCES: Is he?

THERESA: He sings too, so he does.

FRANCES: Who does he go out with?

THERESA: Nobody. They say he's too busy training all the time. Very dedicated fella. His sister says he has no interest in women. Well, let's put that to the test—eh, Frances? [*Giggles*] Hello, Rinty.

YOUNG RINTY: Hello girls.

THERESA: This is Frances.

YOUNG RINTY: Hiya. [*Declaring*] Did anybody ever tell you your face resembles a meadow of roses in the full bloom of summer?

FRANCES: Did anybody ever tell you yours resembles a basinful of wilickes?

[THERESA *stifles a laugh. Then she suddenly jumps up, hiding her drink.*]

THERESA: Oh frig, there's my ma. I'm away d'hide. [*She runs off.*]

YOUNG RINTY: I was wonderin' how I was gonna get rid of her.

FRANCES: [*indignantly*] Whadaya mean?

YOUNG RINTY: I've no seat.

[*He sits beside* FRANCES. *There is an embarrassing moment of silence.*]

YOUNG RINTY: It's Kircubbin then.

FRANCES: Really? I thought it was Paris.

[*Another silence.* YOUNG RINTY *shifts in his seat.*]

FRANCES: You box?

YOUNG RINTY [*enthusiastically*]**:** Did a not tell you about m'last fight? A knocked out—

FRANCES: Have you any brains?

YOUNG RINTY: What?

FRANCES: I've always thought that anybody that boxes must have no brains.

YOUNG RINTY: Who? I get paid for boxin'.

FRANCES: Do ye? Is that not a wee bit like them givin' the stag a feed before the go out huntin' it?

YOUNG RINTY: Where the hell did the get you?

FRANCES: Anyway, I heard something about you.

YOUNG RINTY: What?

FRANCES: Ach, just something.

YOUNG RINTY: Tell me ... tell me.

FRANCES: Is it true you're a boxin' champion but you've never been kissed?

OLD RINTY: In spite of that first sparrin' session on the bus run to Kircubbin, we got on like a house on fire. In fact, we married a couple of years later—Boxin' Day 1938.

[FRANCES *walks across stage carrying a wedding bouquet of flowers.* YOUNG RINTY *follows after her, singing to her.*]

YOUNG RINTY: '... and even though we've drifted far apart
I love you as I loved you
When you were sweet
When you were sweet sixteen.'

OLD RINTY: The following year two very important things happened.

YOUNG RINTY: My first daughter, Martha—

[YOUNG RINTY *and* FRANCES *push a pram across stage.*]

OLD RINTY: —and an energetic wee painter from Austria declared similar ambitions to mine—

YOUNG RINTY: I want to be flyweight boxin' champion of the world—

OLD RINTY: Hitler just wanted d'be champion of the world.

[*Sound of sirens, explosions, etc. Blackout on stage. We see searchlights frantically looking for enemy planes. Sound of planes.*]

People dropped everything and ran to the air-raid shelters.

[*A* MAN *and* WOMAN *run across stage and stop.*]

NED: Oh Jeesis, Tess, I have d'go back d'the house.

TESS [*angrily*]: What?

NED: I have d'go back, a've left m'false teeth in the house.

TESS: Your false teeth! For Jesis sake! What d'ya think it is they're droppin' up there—Paris Buns! [*They run off.*]

OLD RINTY: My oul' mate, Choke-the-dog. He came home one night from the pub—bluttered. He couldn't make it upstairs, so he just tuck his trousers off, threw them over the chile's pram and flopped out on the sofa for the night. An hour later—the sirens went off, an air-raid was on. Choke-the-dog's wife ran down the stairs, threw the chile in the pram—and away like the hammers, to the air-raid shelter. Y'can guess what happened. Choke-the-dog finally got up and went luckin' for his trousers. The wife had them away in the pram. Choke-the-dog had d'run through the streets with not a stitch on. In the meantime, I became an ambulance driver with the ARP. And I saw some sights.

YOUNG RINTY: In Vere Street, not far from where I live. I've just been shovelling the remains of dozens of bodies inda bags.

OLD RINTY: But it wasn't all doom and gloom. ENSA called

[YOUNG RINTY *and* MAXIE, *a guitar player, enter dressed in suits. The sound of bombs etc., increased in background.*]

MAXIE: Where the hell are we, Rinty?

YOUNG RINTY: What does it matter? We volunteered to play anywhere the Armed Forces asked us, didn't we?

MAXIE: Aye, I was thinkin' of places like Biggin Hill, East Anglia ...

maybe even London. Nobody told me I would end up in the middle of France tryin' d'save m'guitar from Hitler's bombs! I'm here playin' 'Begin The Beguine' and Rommel's tellin' us it's 'The End of the End'!

YOUNG RINTY: Here comes the Officer, he'll tell us what's happenin'.

[BRITISH ARMY OFFICER *enters*]

OFFICER: Oh, found you at last.

MAXIE: Unfortunately.

OFFICER: Where the bloody hell have you been?

YOUNG RINTY: Well, we spent two hours on the toilet ...

MAXIE: Then four hours prayin'.

OFFICER: Where's the rest of your band?

YOUNG RINTY: Barricaded in, in the Lord Mayor's cellar.

MAXIE: It just happens d'be a wine cellar.

YOUNG RINTY: Officer, are we on the retreat?

OFFICER: Looks rather like it.

YOUNG RINTY: Well, could we get a fast lorry outta here?

OFFICER: Not a'tall, not a'tall. The retreat will take days. We're having a concert tonight for headquarters staff.

MAXIE: Are y'any good of a singer?

OFFICER: Pardon.

MAXIE: Y'better be, 'cause we're goin' fuckin' home.

OLD RINTY: We got outta France just days before Dunkirk hit the headlines. Then it was back to England—up and down the country singin'.

MAXIE: Yesterday it was the Scots Guards in Sussex, t'day it's the Royal Artillery in Cardiff, where the hell next?

YOUNG RINTY: It could be worse, y'could be a soldier.

MAXIE: No friggin' chance. I'm a fully paid-up member of the Musicians' Union like me father before me. I prefer to throw B-flats and A-minors, not shaggin' hand-grenades. No way. Besides Liverpool needs talent like me.

YOUNG RINTY: I haven't seen my baby in seven months.

MAXIE: What's Belfast like, Rinty?

YOUNG RINTY: Ach, it's alright. We have a lotta problems over religion.

MAXIE: Well, we've got Catholics and Protestants in Liverpool. They all believe in it alright but nobody bothers to practice it.

YOUNG RINTY: In Belfast it's the opposite. Everybody practices but nobody believes.

MAXIE: When this war's over I'm goin' back to Liverpool to start the best band this country's ever seen. Artie Shaw won't be in it.

YOUNG RINTY: The least you could do is ask him.

MAXIE: I mean his band won't be as good as mine. You can be in it, Rinty.

YOUNG RINTY: Thanks very much, Maxie, but—

MAXIE: What are y'gonna do after the war? You used to be a boxer, didn'y ya?

YOUNG RINTY: Yeah, about three hundred years ago. If somebody would invent a new sport where y'boxed and sang at the same time, I'd be a millionaire.

MAXIE: Well, which do you prefer—boxin' or singing?

YOUNG RINTY: Singin'. But how many people can earn a livin' at just singin'?

MAXIE: Al Jolson.

[YOUNG RINTY *gives* MAXIE *a 'don't-be-smart' look.*]

YOUNG RINTY: I don't know. Sometimes a hate boxin' but a know that if a went at it ... if a went at it ... serious like ... a could earn a lotta money at it.

MAXIE: So I wanna have the best band in the world and you wanna make a lotta money? What happened to the music, Rinty?

YOUNG RINTY: Ah ... the music. Who really needs it, Maxie?

MAXIE: Who needs it? We all friggin' need it. Look at us? What are we doin' now? Men are going out to kill—they need music! They come back after killing—they need more music! In our lives— painting, literature—we mightn't think it—but we need all these things. It's all music.

YOUNG RINTY: Well, how often do most of us get these, these 'necessary' things? This music? Where I come from there's very little music. Music comes after poverty, Maxie, not durin'. So if it's a choice between music and boxin'—boxin' wins every time.

MAXIE [*sadly*]: I don't like to hear you say that.

[YOUNG RINTY *prepares to go.*]

YOUNG RINTY: Anyway, at the minute young men aren't allowed to do anything as cissy as boxin'—they're needed for killin'. Time d'make some more music, Maxie oul' mate—let's go.

MAXIE: Yeah. Time to soothe another regiment of troubled minds. And Rinty? [YOUNG RINTY *stops*] After the war, try and stay with the music.

OLD RINTY: But, there was really only one opponent worth fightin' and that was the wee Austrian painter. In the meantime, the infrequent visits home hadn't been completely unproductive. My second daughter, Rosetta, was born. And while I was the happiest man in the world, Frank McAloran wasn't.

[*McAloran's Gym.* FRANK *is tidying up for the night, collecting boxing gloves, sweeping the floor etc.* YOUNG RINTY *enters.*]

YOUNG RINTY: Y'couldn't train a cat d'lick milk.

[FRANK *turns around surprised.*]

FRANK: Rinty.

YOUNG RINTY: How's the form, Frank?

FRANK: Not bad, not bad. And yourself?

YOUNG RINTY: Couldn't be better. Y'know me—'If in doubt, laugh.'

FRANK: How's the kids?

YOUNG RINTY: Great. Two wee wreckers. 'Is there life after kids?'— that's what I wanna know.

FRANK: What has ye up here?

YOUNG RINTY: Am a not allowed d'call in and see m'manager?

FRANK: Manager?

YOUNG RINTY: What are ya then?

FRANK: I manage boxers Rinty, not dancehall crooners.

YOUNG RINTY: What am I?

FRANK: Good question.

YOUNG RINTY: What d'hell are you on about, Frank?

FRANK: A'm just statin' facts.

YOUNG RINTY: What facts?

FRANK: A told ya. I manage boxers, not entertainers.

YOUNG RINTY: I do both.

FRANK: Y'can't. Nobody can.

YOUNG RINTY: There's been a war on.

FRANK: It hasn't stopped Bunty Doran.

YOUNG RINTY: What about Bunty Doran?

FRANK: He's Flyweight Champion of Ireland, that's what.

YOUNG RINTY: I knocked out Joe Meikle last year.

FRANK: And tap-danced at the Empire the rest of the year.

YOUNG RINTY: A have d'earn a livin'.

FRANK: So does Jackie Paterson.

YOUNG RINTY: Who cares about Jackie Paterson!

FRANK: He's earnin' a livin'. A good livin'. He's Flyweight Champion of the World.

YOUNG RINTY: So?

FRANK: So? What are you champion of? Little Corporation Street? You're the best flyweight in the whole of Little Corporation Street, is that it?

[YOUNG RINTY *stands silenced, hurt.*]

FRANK: Excuse me Rinty, a've d'lock up.

[*He brushes past* YOUNG RINTY *carrying the box.*]

YOUNG RINTY: You think I could beat Bunty?

FRANK: And Jackie Paterson. [YOUNG RINTY *shakes his head, disbelieving.*] But you'd have d'give it everything. No singin', no dancin', no gallivantin'—just work, work, work, and dedication.

YOUNG RINTY: What makes you think I could beat these men?

FRANK: Because yiv got that there. [FRANK *holds up his right fist and shakes it.*] Rinty, yiv the hardest right hand in the world at the minute. And what I would give d'see it inside a glove instead of holdin' a bloody microphone.

[YOUNG RINTY *again lapses into silence.* FRANK *moves to exit.*]

YOUNG RINTY: Could y'get me Bunty?

FRANK: Before the year's out. Two or three warm-ups, then Bunty.

YOUNG RINTY: A take it it's still the buckets a cold water?

FRANK: Still the buckets a cold water. And by the way, we've a new young fella here d'spar ya, who's one of the best prospects a've ever seen.

YOUNG RINTY: Who's that?

FRANK: Eddie McCullough.

YOUNG RINTY: A'll be here the marra night.

[FRANK *exits.* YOUNG RINTY *wanders across the stage.*]

OLD RINTY: Frances never said anything but, like most women, her instinct told her to hate boxin'.

[FRANCES *enters.*]

FRANCES: There was a man here wants y'to go and sing in Dublin.

YOUNG RINTY: Tell him d'go and get stuffed.

FRANCES: What?

YOUNG RINTY: How would you like d'be rich?

FRANCES: Lovely.

YOUNG RINTY: How would you like to live in a big house?

FRANCES: I like it here.

YOUNG RINTY: I'm gonna transform our lives.

FRANCES: Were you drinkin'?

YOUNG RINTY: A've just taken a major decision t'day Frances, a'm gonna be a boxer.

FRANCES: Y'were definitely drinkin'.

YOUNG RINTY: I'm serious.

FRANCES: Sure, yiv been boxin' since before I knew ya.

YOUNG RINTY: Aye, but this time I'm serious. A'm gonna be Champion of the World.

FRANCES: Is that right? Well, at this minute we've no supper, no breakfast, the childer need new clothes, the house is fallin' down round us and we owe a wee Jew Boy thirty pound.

YOUNG RINTY: Well ... at least we're not poverty stricken!

FRANCES: That's always your answer.

YOUNG RINTY: What?

FRANCES: A joke. Everytime you're faced with something difficult or something you don't like—y'take the easy way out, y'make a joke, laugh about it.

YOUNG RINTY [*singing*]: 'Don't laugh at me 'cause I'm a fool ...'

FRANCES: Exactly.

YOUNG RINTY: It's just the way I am, Frances. I can't change it.

FRANCES: It's time y'did. The war's over nigh. Other men are runnin' around gettin' themselves fixed up with good jobs. Thinkin' about their families. What are you doin'? What have you got yourself fixed up with? Good steady, secure, well-paid employment as a—boxer? No wonder I despair at times.

YOUNG RINTY: You're not listenin' to me, Frances. I *will* be earnin' good money. Didn't a get fifty quid for the Joe Curran fight in Liverpool?

FRANCES: That's about eight weeks' wages. What happens for the next eight weeks?

YOUNG RINTY: I'm pushin' McAloran d'get me as many fights as he can.

FRANCES: Rinty, only for me goin' out and workin', we'd be even worse off than we are.

YOUNG RINTY: You wait, you just wait. It's gonna get better. A have the Bunty Doran fight comin' up. After that, it's the top. You watch me, Frances Thompson. Anything that went before, doesn't count. This is the new me. I'm gonna train harder than any man's ever trained before. Every day. Every single day. [*He turns around and looks at* FRANCES. *She stares back at him, wondering if what he's saying could possibly come true.*]

OLD RINTY: So the war ended. The wee painter wouldn't be doin' any more paintin' and I had learned three things.

First one was: that while I had been concentratin' on singin' m'way through the war, Jackie Paterson—the wee fella that knocked me out at the Oval in 1938—was now top of the heap. Second thing was: that's what I wanted to be. More than anything else in the world, I wanted to be up there. I wanted d'fly high, I wanted d'be the eagle among birds, the mountain among hills, the king among men—the best flyweight in the whole world. Third thing was: if a didn't, Frances would kick me out in the street.

[EDDIE MCCULLOUGH *enters trailing a large log onstage. He drops it beside* OLD RINTY *and exits.* OLD RINTY *lifts the log and backs onto centre-stage. He drops the log.*]

OLD RINTY: Meantime, there was a problematic, eight-stone bundle of perpetual motion who was goin' d'bed with me every night.

YOUNG RINTY: His name is Bunty Doran. Every night a go d'bed it's Bunty, Bunty, Bunty. [*Taps his finger against his temple.*]

OLD RINTY: And every day it was the Cavehill and young Eddie McCullough.

[EDDIE MCCULLOUGH *enters with two trestles. They place the log on the trestles and beging sawing logs with a large band-saw.*]

YOUNG RINTY: C'mon McCullough, you're not pushin'.

EDDIE: I am, I am.

YOUNG RINTY: Faster! Faster! [YOUNG RINTY *stops.*] Okay, that'll do us for a while. [*The two men take a breather.*]

EDDIE: Wouldn't it be a laugh, if after all this, Bunty knocked you out in the first round?

YOUNG RINTY: There's about as much chance of that happenin' as there is of Hitler bein' alive and well, and knockin' about McAloran's Gym disguised as Boxer Hall.

EDDIE: I read that.

YOUNG RINTY: Read what?

EDDIE: That Hitler was still alive.

YOUNG RINTY: Rubbish.

EDDIE: It says that Hitler was still alive and livin' in the Vatican as a top advisor to the Pope.

YOUNG RINTY: Where'd y'read that?

EDDIE: *The Protestant News Letter.*

[YOUNG RINTY *nods his head knowingly.*]

YOUNG RINTY: Know what's wrong with you, Eddie son? You read too much.

EDDIE: Y'learn things by readin'.

YOUNG RINTY: That's alright, but y'have d'live too. Gettin' all your knowledge from books is like learnin' d'drive a car on country roads, sooner or later you have d'go into the city.

EDDIE: But when I read I can escape from Belfast ... Ireland. I can spend a whole week in New York if the book lasts me that long. France, Brazil, China ... books can take y'anywhere.

YOUNG RINTY: Well, make sure and get a book d'take y'to Ballycastle on Friday night. It mighten be as exotic as Brazil or China but we're booked d'do a Boxin' Exhibition up there, remember?

EDDIE: How did you know I was thinkin' about that?

YOUNG RINTY: Why?

EDDIE: I can't go.

YOUNG RINTY: Why not?

EDDIE: I'm playin' at a concert in the Ulster Hall on Friday night.

YOUNG RINTY: Playin' what?

EDDIE: The violin.

YOUNG RINTY: The violin! Holy frig! Who ever heard of of a violin-playin', book-readin' prize fighter? A suppose you'll be actin' in a Shakespeare play next?

EDDIE: Music's important, Rinty.

YOUNG RINTY: Don't you start.

EDDIE: Whadaya mean?

YOUNG RINTY: You remind me of a guy I knew in ENSA. He went on about 'needin' music too.

EDDIE: But we do. Music is to us what steam is to a train. A neccessary release.

YOUNG RINTY: I thought Maxie was away in the head, Eddie, but you're a complete buffalo's arse.

EDDIE [*moves to go*]: Right, I have to go now. Violin practice.

YOUNG RINTY: Waita minute, waita minute. You were reared in the New Lodge Road—how come you learned to play the violin and I didn't?

EDDIE: I was taught. Music lessons. Paid for by my mother.

YOUNG RINTY: My mother couldn't afford d'send me d'music lessons.

EDDIE: Neither could mine. So she stopped goin' to the pictures. She said that me havin' music in my life was more important than her havin' romance in hers.

YOUNG RINTY: So when am a gonna hear you playin' this violin? [YOUNG RINTY *gets up.*]

EDDIE: Right nigh if you want?

YOUNG RINTY: You have it with ya?

EDDIE: Over in the barn.

YOUNG RINTY: Bring it over.

EDDIE: No, no, I'll tell you what a'll do. You sit here. I'll stand on the side of that hill and we'll just let the music sweep over the Cavehill. Don't move.

[EDDIE *runs off. Soon, we hear the violin being stroked as Eddie readies himself for playing. Then a melody from* Carmen *sweeps over the Cavehill.* YOUNG RINTY *admires the music.*]

YOUNG RINTY: A wonder does Bunty Doran play the violin?

OLD RINTY: The prospect of the Rinty/Bunty fight was the talk of Belfast. It even divided families—

JIMMY: Rinty Munegin's not in the same class.

PADDY: Bollicks!

JIMMY: Bunty'll murder'im.

PADDY: Who? Bunty's a big girl's blouse.

JIMMY [*losing temper*]: Wanna go outside and say that?

PADDY: Jimmy, I'm your brother.

JIMMY: You'll be m'dead brother, any more remarks like that.

PADDY: Jimmy, I'm a Rinty man.

JIMMY: And I'm a Bunty man and it's your round.

OLD RINTY: We built a trainin' camp at the back of a farm at the bottom of the Cavehill. It was owned by a wee woman called Caulfield. She used to keep a goat and made sure I had my bottle of goat's milk every day.

[MRS. CAULFIELD *hands* YOUNG RINTY *bottle of milk.*]

MRS. CAULFIELD: There y'are, Rinty. Here's your milk and a pray d'God it gives ye the strength d'murder all round ye the next time y'step inda the ring.

YOUNG RINTY: Thanks, Mrs. Caulfield. [*She exits.* YOUNG RINTY *drinks the milk.*]

OLD RINTY: At times the camp resembled Royal Avenue as McAloran trekked up reporters, photographers, promoters, broadcasters, businessmen, you name it.

[FRANK MCALORAN *enters with* BOB GARDINER *and* PHOTOGRAPHER.]

FRANK: Rinty, y'know Bob Gardiner, the promoter?

YOUNG RINTY: Hiya doin', Bob?

BOB: Good d'see y'Rinty.

[PHOTOGRAPHER *lines up a picture as the men shake hands.*]

PHOTOGRAPHER: Look this way please, gentlemen.

[*He continues to take pictures as the men talk.*]

BOB: Well, tip-top shape, Rinty?

YOUNG RINTY: Best shape of m'life. A ran up the Bellvue Steps a hundred-and-twenty-five times yesterday without stoppin'— backwards! After a beat Bunty a want y'd'line up a fight with Buck Alec and his lion. [*The men laugh.*]

BOB: The word from Bunty's camp is that he's rearin' d'go.

FRANK: Go where? There's only one place Bunty's goin'—that's the deck.

BOB: He's the bookies' favourite.

PHOTOGRAPHER: Rinty? [YOUNG RINTY *turns to camera, camera clicks*]

FRANK: Ah, but they don't know the new Rinty.

BOB: You're confident then?

YOUNG RINTY: Confident? I've already selected the song a'm gonna sing after a win.

BOB: You're gonna sing in the ring?

YOUNG RINTY: Why not? A'm not allowed d'sing outside it, eh Frank?

OLD RINTY: The excitement mounted. The bookies were indeed makin' Bunty a clear favourite and some of my own best friends left no doubts where their loyalties lay.

[CHOKE-THE-DOG *enters.*]

CHOKE-THE-DOG: Ya Billy Rinty, there y'are, a've been luckin' all over for ye.

YOUNG RINTY: What's the problem, Choke-the-dog?

CHOKE-THE-DOG: A'm luckin' the loan of a poun'.

YOUNG RINTY: You're in luck.

[YOUNG RINTY *takes pound note from pocket and give it to* CHOKE-THE-DOG.]

CHOKE-THE-DOG: Oh thanks, Rinty, y'saved m'life.

YOUNG RINTY: Something wrong, Choke-the-dog? Sumpin' in the house?

CHOKE-THE-DOG: Oh no, nothin' like that. A just need a poun' d'put on Bunty for the big fight.

YOUNG RINTY: Put on Bunty!

OLD RINTY: But I did have some very loyal supporters. Like Mrs. Graham, a wee woman from the Newtownards Road.

MRS. GRAHAM [*singing*]: 'A had a wee dog and a learned it d'sing, Rintyboo!

A had a wee dog and a learned it d'sing Rintyboo!

—A had a wee dog and a learned it d'sing

Knock wee Bunty outta the ring

Eeky, Beeky Rintyboo!'

[*Shouts*] Up Rinty! [*She approaches* YOUNG RINTY.]

Well, Rinty son, are y'gonna win?

YOUNG RINTY: 'Course I am, Mrs. Graham.

MRS. GRAHAM Don't you be one bit afeared of him. [YOUNG RINTY *smiles.*] Giv 'im one, two. And if that doesn't work [*whispers*] Giv 'im one in the balls! [*Shouts*] Up Rinty! A haven't missed a Rinty Munegin fight yit!

OLD RINTY: In the Ulster Hall dressing-room before the fight a had a few minutes d'm'self. Only a boxer knows what sort of thoughts go through your head at that point, the main one is fear, fear of losing, fear of being disgraced, not that you would reveal this to anyone. For me, this fight was the big one. The Irish Flyweight Title. If I won this, I'd be on my way up. If I lost—

who knows? Lorry-drivin', emptyin' bins, the dole. D'take
m'mind off things I used d'play the mouth-organ.
[YOUNG RINTY *is sitting on a table playing the harmonica. He is wearing
a dressing-gown.* FRANK MCALORAN *enters.*]

FRANK: Alright, Rinty?

YOUNG RINTY: Fine, fine.

OLD RINTY: I was shitin' m'self.

FRANK: How's the nerves?

OLD RINTY: In bits.

YOUNG RINTY: No problem.

FRANK: The place is packed.

OLD RINTY: Any chance of gettin' me outta this?

YOUNG RINTY: That's great.

OLD RINTY: Is there a back door?

FRANK: Bunty just made the weight and no more. So there'll be no
power in his punches.

OLD RINTY: Bunty Doran threw more punches than any boxer I knew.

FRANK: He misses mosta the time anyway.

OLD RINTY: Frank had me convinced a was boxin' the Venus de Milo.

FRANK: Anything y'need?

OLD RINTY: Yeah, cancel the fight, Frank. Tell them m'ma was
knocked down by a horse-and-cart on the way down d'the fight.
Tell them anything, just cancel it.

FRANK: Need a drink of anything? [YOUNG RINTY *shakes his head.*]
Right, let's get warmed up. A bit of skippin'. [YOUNG RINTY *skips.*]

OLD RINTY: One of the problems boxers have—I had anyway—was
gettin' motivated d'hurt somebody you'd no reason d'hurt.
There is only one reason why men do it—money. Forget the
claptrap—glory comes a poor second. Frank McAloran was a
master of subtlety.

FRANK: Right Rinty, y'know what y'have d'do d'night? [YOUNG RINTY
stares straight ahead.] Kill Bunty Doran. [YOUNG RINTY *looks at*
FRANK *sharply.*] He's the champion. If he beats you tonight, his
next fight is against Jackie Paterson for the World Title. Do you
know how much his purse will be? £5,000. Just think for a
minute, what you could do with £5,000. [*Pause*] What age is your
youngest wee girl, Rosetta? Two, three? Just imagine, just think,
what you could do for your Martha and Rosetta, with that sorta
money? [*Pause*] When you go out inda that ring Rinty, have a
good look at what's there. It won't be Bunty Doran you're luckin
at. It'll be your entire future. Your kids' future.

[BUNTY *enters,* OLD RINTY *acts as his trainer, rubbing his shoulders and neck.*]

OLD RINTY: I knew Bunty well. We were reared a couple of streets away from each other.

BUNTY: The first time I remember Rinty was at school in Donegall Street. Durin' lunch-eyre, he used d'take a brand new motorbike out of a car showroom beside the *Irish News* offices and drive it round the square. He brought it back—to the showroom windy without the owner even knowin' it was away. I used d'say d'myself, 'Thon fella's mad.'

OLD RINTY: Bunty was a good boxer.

YOUNG RINTY: He's a tough wee bastard.

BUNTY: Rinty is more of a technical boxer, a counter-puncher.

OLD RINTY: Bunty didn't know the meanin' of the words 'go back'.

YOUNG RINTY: From the minute he entered the ring til the minute he left—it was go, go, go.

BUNTY: I was totally confident.

FRANK: Okay, Rinty, ready d'go?

OLD RINTY: Remember, Bunty. Don't let him rest. Torment him, torment him.

FRANK: This is it, Rinty. The big one—it's you or him. Kill him. Alright? Kill him.

OLD RINTY: Torment him, torment him.

OFFICIAL: Seconds out! Round One!

[*The bell sounds, the two men face each other. They prowl around each other.*]

OLD RINTY: I looked inda Bunty's eyes. It was ridiculous. I said—

YOUNG RINTY: Why am I fightin' you?

BUNTY: I don't know.

YOUNG RINTY: Do you know who you are?

BUNTY: The last time a lucked in the mirror a was Bunty Doran.

YOUNG RINTY: You're not.

BUNTY: No?

YOUNG RINTY: You're £5,000. Frank says you're not a person, you're £5,000.

BUNTY: C'mon Rinty, we're supposed d'be gettin' stuck in here.

YOUNG RINTY: Why do we have d'do this? Why am I fightin' you?

BUNTY: I don't know.

YOUNG RINTY: But I know you. We grew up in the same district.

BUNTY: I suppose we're earnin' a livin'.

YOUNG RINTY: That's it, that's just it. Why do we have d'earn a livin' by tryin' d'knock the shite outiv each other?

BUNTY: Well, I work as a lorry driver and that wouldn't keep y'on fegs.

YOUNG RINTY: Is it the district we were brought up in?

BUNTY: Not really. I've boxed guys from the Shankill, Short Strand—all over the place.

YOUNG RINTY: Is it Belfast then?

BUNTY: I've boxed in Newcastle, Glasgow, Liverpool.

YOUNG RINTY: What is it, then?

BUNTY: Rinty, luck, we have d'make a show here.

YOUNG RINTY: Put it this way. If we grew up the Malone Road somewhere and went d'Campbell College, would we be in here nigh behavin' like this ... like wild animals?

BUNTY: We're gettin' paid.

YOUNG RINTY: So do university lecturers.

[*The bell sounds. Both boxers go back to their corners.*]

OLD RINTY: Legend has it that I scraped the first round. But only just. Both of us were still gettin' the measure of each other.

FRANK: Well done, Rinty. Well done. Watch his right hook, keep an eye on his right hook. He's tryin d'catch ya over your left.

OLD RINTY: Well done, Bunty. Well done. Watch his right hand, whatever y'do watch his right hand.

FRANK: Step it up this round. Throw more right hands. He's there for the takin'

OLD RINTY: Take it to him nigh, Bunty. Get in close. He doesn't like it in close.

OFFICAL: Seconds out! Round Two!

[*The bell sounds and the two men face each other again.*]

YOUNG RINTY: Bunty, do you have much music in your life?

[BUNTY *stops and stares at* YOUNG RINTY.]

BUNTY: You're a fuckin' nut.

YOUNG RINTY: Serious.

BUNTY: What?

YOUNG RINTY: Is there many flowers in your life?

BUNTY: Aye, our backyard in Nelson Street is a riot of colour.

YOUNG RINTY: Do you know that music is as important to us as fresh drinking water? Flowers are as important as bacon and egg?

BUNTY: Well, a'd hate d'come home hungry from a days work, and the wife set me down a plate a freshly cut geraniums and played Joe Loss on the gramophone.

YOUNG RINTY: Bunty, do you ever dream?

BUNTY: Whadaya mean, do I ever dream? Of course a dream.

YOUNG RINTY: What about?

BUNTY: Fuck, I can't remember, I'm supposed d'be concentratin' on tryin' d'kill you.

YOUNG RINTY: What was your last dream?

BUNTY: A was in a Turkish Bath.

YOUNG RINTY: What were y'doin' in a Turkish Bath?

BUNTY: Tryin' d'lose weight for this friggin' fight, whadaya think!

YOUNG RINTY: And what happened?

BUNTY: A beautiful woman came in.

YOUNG RINTY: And?

BUNTY: She came over to me.

YOUNG RINTY: And?

BUNTY: She took my hand.

YOUNG RINTY: And?

BUNTY: She says, 'Bunty let me take you away from all this'. I says, 'A can't, a've d'fight Rinty Munegin and a need the money'. She says, 'It's alright, I have plenty of money.' I says, 'What about Rinty, he needs the money.' She says, 'It's alright, Rinty's just got a university lecturer's job.' [*The bell sounds and the two men return to their corners.*]

OLD RINTY: Bunty definitely won the second round. In fact, he caught me with a great punch and it hurt like hell. It was every bit as tough as I knew it would be.

FRANK: What did a tell ya, what did a tell ya? He caught y'with the left hook.

OLD RINTY: You've got 'im, you've got him. He'll not last another round.

FRANK: Remember, Rinty. You're starin' at your future here. Lorry-driver, binman or Champion of the World. It's up d'you. Throw the right, keep throwin' the right.

OLD RINTY: Right, Bunty son, go out and finish it.

FRANK: Throw the right, Rinty—hit 'im w'the right!

OLD RINTY: Finish it, Bunty, finish it!

FRANK: Kill him, kill him!

OLD RINTY: Knock 'im out, knock 'im out!

OFFICIAL: Seconds out! Round Three!

[*The bell rings. The two men confront each other.*]

YOUNG RINTY: Hyre many kids have y'nigh, Bunty?

BUNTY: Two.

YOUNG RINTY: Same as m'self.

BUNTY: And the have d'be fed every day.

YOUNG RINTY: Well, at least the last election has brought the changes.

BUNTY: We got rida Churchill and the Tories.

[*The two men sing loudly together, vibrantly.*]

BUNTY and **YOUNG RINTY:** 'Rule Britannia, Britannia rules the waves. Britons never never, never shall be slaves ...'

YOUNG RINTY: A wonder what this new crowd's gonna be like?

BUNTY: Maybe now, things'll be better for the workin' man.

YOUNG RINTY: We'll have d'wait and see. There's never been a real Labour government before.

BUNTY and **YOUNG RINTY** [*singing*]: 'So raise the scarlet standard high
Beneath its fold we'll live and die
Though cowards flinch and traitors sneer
We'll keep the red flag flying here ...'

BUNTY: And over here the same crowd's won again.

BUNTY and **YOUNG RINTY:** The Unionists!
[*They sing*] 'Sure me father wore it in his youth
In the bygone days of yore
And it's on the twelth I love to wear
The sash my father wore.'

YOUNG RINTY: A don't see much change in any part of Ireland, do you?

BUNTY: What, that Dublin crowd?

BUNTY and **YOUNG RINTY** [*singing*]: 'We're on the one road,
Sharing the one road
We're on the road to God knows where
We're on the one road, swinging along
Singing the Soldiers Song ...'

YOUNG RINTY: A don't think it matters to the likes a me and you Bunty, who's in power. We'll still have d'do this.

BUNTY: We're flyweights, we could always take up ballet dancing.
[*The bell sounds. The two men return to their corners.*]

OLD RINTY: The third round was the toughest yet. I hurt him and he had me on the ropes a couple of times. The pace was electric. To say that Bunty was tough was to say that grass was a greenish colour.

FRANK: Well done, Rinty, that's more like it. You've hurt 'im, you've hurt 'im.

OLD RINTY: Well done, Bunty, that's more like it. You've hurt 'im, you've hurt 'im.

FRANK: Hyre do y'feel?

YOUNG RINTY: Great

OLD RINTY: Hyre do y'feel?

BUNTY: Great

FRANK: I think he's there for the takin'. He's ready d'go.

OLD RINTY: I think he's there for the takin'. He's ready d'go.

FRANK: Keep proddin' out the left hand, wait your chance and— bang—in w'the right hand and Bob's-your-uncle.

OLD RINTY: Keep the combinations goin', then—bang—up with the left hook and Bob's-your-uncle.

FRANK: Okay, Rinty? This is your fight. You need this fight. You're nothin' if you lose this one.

OLD RINTY: Okay, Bunty? This is your fight. Win this one and it's the World Title next time out.

FRANK: Do it for the family. Do it for your wee daughters. Do it, Rinty, go out there and do it.

OLD RINTY: Do it for the family. Do it for your wee childer. Do it, Bunty, go out there and do it.

FRANK: Kill 'im, Rinty, kill 'im!

OLD RINTY: Knock 'im out, Bunty, knock 'im out!

FRANK: Go on, knock his head off his shoulders!

OLD RINTY: Go on, tear 'im apart limb from limb!

OFFICIAL: Seconds out! The fourth and final round!

[*The bell sounds.*]

BUNTY: [*shouting off*] Hold on a minute! This is a scheduled 15 rounder, what's this about the 'fourth and final round?'

OFFICIAL: I'm only reading off the script!

[*The men face each other.*]

YOUNG RINTY: Okay, Bunty? This is where I touch for you with a peach of a right hand.

BUNTY: A never even saw it comin'.

YOUNG RINTY: That was the general idea.

BUNTY: I ended up in hospital for observation.

YOUNG RINTY: So did I. That time you hit me in the second, left me with a hairline fracture of the jaw.

BUNTY: What a way d'earn a livin', eh?

YOUNG RINTY: After I knock you out a'm gonna sing 'The Gypsy'— is that alright?

BUNTY: Sing whatever the hell y'like.

[*The two men stand toe to toe slugging it out.* BUNTY *steps back.* YOUNG RINTY *hits him with a right hand.* BUNTY *goes down.* OLD RINTY *goes to his aid. A microphone comes down and* YOUNG RINTY *sings* 'The Gypsy'.]

YOUNG RINTY [*singing*]: 'In a quaint caravan
There's a lady they call the Gypsy
She can look in the future and drive away all your fears
Everything will come right if you only believe the Gypsy
She could tell at a glance that my heart was so full of tears ... '

Singing and lights fade. Black-out.

ACT TWO

Onstage, a six-month old baby lies in a pram. YOUNG RINTY *enters shaking a baby's bottle filled with milk.*

YOUNG RINTY: A'm comin', a'm comin', a'm comin'! There. [*He gives the baby the bottle.*] How's that? Alright? No more cryin' outta ye, nigh? [*He shakes the pram gently.* OLD RINTY *enters.*]

OLD RINTY: 1948. Third chile, Colette. Frances hada wait til I got back from m'mornin' runs up the Cavehill before she could get out d'the shops. The one thing havin' young children does—it forces y'd'get your life in perspective.

YOUNG RINTY [*to* CHILD]: Nigh, tell me something, kiddo. Am I gonna get a sleep d'night or are you gonna gurn the night again? I need m'sleep, bucko. Do you not know your daddy's a boxer? I have d'train like hell—every day. That means a need d'be asleep b'ten o'clock—and up at *six*. Do you know that? Okay, lets make a deal. If you let me sleep at nights—I'll win the World Title just for you. No, better still. A'm gonna win it whether you let me sleep or not. A'm gonna win it for you and Reta and Martha. How's that? All our lives are gonna change after t'night. I'll make sure of that. You've never heard of a wee man called Jackie Paterson, have ya?

[FRANCES *enters.*]

FRANCES: There's a telegram. Did you not see that lyin' in the hall?

YOUNG RINTY: A telegram! Must be something about the fight.

[YOUNG RINTY *proceeds to open the telegram and reads it.*]

OLD RINTY: It was over two years since a beat Bunty Doran. A'd fought and beat the best the threw at me, including a non-title fight win over—guess who?—Jackie Paterson. But, still he wouldn't put up his World Title against me. Frustration was beginnin' to set in when—

REPORTER: Are you going to listen to the big fight tonight?

TAMATA: Yiss.

REPORTER: Who do you think will win?

TAMATA: Rinty Munegin will knock his ballicks in!

[REPORTER *is stunned. He looks at the tape recorder and back to* TAMATA. *He turns the tape recorder off.*]

REPORTER: You didn't use that language when I asked you that same question a few minutes ago.

TAMATA: A just ... a just thought of it there nigh.

[REPORTER *is exasperated. He switches on the tape recorder and speaks into the microphone.*]

REPORTER: So I'll be here throughout the night, to soak up the atmosphere and bring you firsthand reports from the home of Rinty Monaghan in Belfast's dockland.

OLD RINTY: And just like in the Bunty Doran fight, Choke-the-dog came luckin' for me.

CHOKE-THE-DOG: Ah Rinty, there y'are. A've been luckin' all over for ya.

YOUNG RINTY: What's up?

CHOKE-THE-DOG: Y'wouldn't have 18 shillins on ye?

YOUNG RINTY: What for?

CHOKE-THE-DOG: A've been runnin back and forward d'the pawn and a've raised four poun', two shillin's. A need 18 shillin's d'make it up d'a fiver.

YOUNG RINTY: Y'musta pawned a hell of a lot d'make four poun', two shillin's, Choke-the-dog?

CHOKE-THE-DOG: Ach not much. Just her weddin' dress, her ma's weddin' dress, every sheet and blanket there was in the house, the clock, the wireless and three pairs a her ma's knickers! [*Pause*] He wouldn't take our tin bath, said there was holes in it.

YOUNG RINTY: Whadaya need all this money for, anyway?

CHOKE-THE-DOG: D'put on the fight, whadaya think?

YOUNG RINTY: Who y'backin', me or Paterson?

CHOKE-THE-DOG: Ah no, it's not your fight, Rinty. You're a cert for that, no problem. This one's between her ma and da! Know the way her ma and da's seperated? Well, he came back last night when she wasn't there and set fire d'the sofa before smashin' every windy in the house. I've bet Roofspace McCrudden a fiver that we'll be attendin' his funeral before the week's out. That's why a need the fiver.

YOUNG RINTY: But if you think I'm a dead cert Choke-the-dog, why not put the fiver on me?

CHOKE-THE-DOG: Ah nigh a didn't say y'were a *dead* cert. You've a
reasonable chance [*Shiftily looks at the ground*] ... it's just that I
know her da will be dead by Saturday. [YOUNG RINTY *gives* CHOKE-
THE-DOG *18 shillings.*]

OLD RINTY: In the meantime, the hour of the fight had arrived.
Eleven thousand people crammed into the King's Hall. The
streets of Belfast were deserted. Everybody was indoors gathered
round their wireless sets.

[REPORTER *and bar customers sit around a wireless set.*]

COMMENTATOR: As we all know Paterson was late arriving in Belfast
today amid speculation about his weight problems, but he's here
tonight—he's here alright, and so are thousands of others, here
at Belfast's King's Hall, where the atmosphere is ... and here
comes Rinty Monaghan! ... [*The men cheer and shout. The King's
Hall crowd roar.*] ... the pride of Belfast, the singing boxer with
the lethal right hand, Rinty Monaghan is in the ring! [*More
roaring and chees*]

OLD RINTY: When I climbed into the ring that night, I was strangely
confident. I was content within myself. This was my chance to fly
high. Like an eagle among birds, a mountain among hills, a king
among men. This was my chance. From the openin' bell, I went
at Paterson like a man possessed. [*We hear the roars of the crowd.
Then, from the pram baby* COLETTE *begins to cry.* OLD RINTY *goes over
and takes her in his arms, tenderly.*] There, there, there. Just
another half-an-hour or so and your da won't be just John
Joseph Monaghan from the backstreets—but Rinty Monaghan,
champion   of   the   whole   world,   from   Melbourne
d'Massachusetts, Mexico d'Manchester. It'll be your da.

[REPORTER *in Dockland pub.*]

REPORTER: And after three rounds here, the supporters of Rinty
Monaghan are still as confident as ever. [*He turns to* TAMATA]
How do you feel the fight's going after three rounds? [TAMATA
slips REPORTER *a drink.*]

TAMATA: Well, he put Paterson down in the second, right? He
caught him a whopper—bop—down Paterson went. And I think
he's finished. Rinty's gonna murder 'im.

REPORTER: Thank you, and so here in Belfast's Dockland—

[TAMATA *leans over to microphone.*]

TAMATA: Could I say something else?

REPORTER: Excuse me, Rinty's fans are extremely excited—

TAMATA: Rinty's gonna fuckin' kill 'im.

[REPORTER *quickly turns off the recorder and puts his hand to his head.*]

OLD RINTY: The fight was goin' exactly accordin' d'plan but I still had d'be careful. Paterson was the best two-handed knock-out man since Benny Lynch. I had d'wait m'chance.

[*The men in the bar sitting around the wireless listen to the commentary.*]

COMMENTATOR: We're near the end of Round Six now and if anything, Paterson looks to be getting stronger. He's coming forward more often now—and he rocks Monaghan with a right!—and another right! These are anxious moments for Monaghan's fans here in the King's Hall. [*The bell sounds.*] And at the end of the round Paterson walks, almost runs, back to his corner ...

OLD RINTY: I remember goin' back to m'stool at the end of Round Six and McAloran was shoutin' instructions at me—and I looked across at Paterson—and all I could think of was her. [*Indicating* COLETTE, *still in his arms*] I had d'win. This was it. I wasn't goin' d'lose this fight.

[*He looks lovingly at* COLETTE. REPORTER *is talking to* TAMATA. TAMATA *gives him another whiskey.*]

REPORTER: Is that alright? You don't mind.

TAMATA: No, that's dead on. From nigh on, when you ask me a question—no cursin'.

REPORTER: Please.

TAMATA: Certainly, sorry, sorry about that.

REPORTER: That's alright.

TAMATA: No cursin', no swear words.

[REPORTER *turns on the tape recorder.*]

REPORTER: Welcome back to the heart of Belfast Dockland. Round Seven is just about to begin and the excitement here is almost unbearable. [*To* TAMATA] Paterson had a very good sixth round, do you think he's getting stronger?

TAMATA: He is, but I don't think it'll last. I think Rinty will step up a gear soon.

REPORTER: That was a terrific punch Paterson caught him with in the last round.

TAMATA: No it fuuu ... Not a'tall. Rinty's as strong as a bull. You watch the next couple a rounds. [REPORTER *gives* TAMATA *the thumbs up.*]

REPORTER: Okay, there you have it, Rinty Monaghan's fans are as confident as ever. The atmosphere here in this Dockland public house is certainly something I've never witnessed before. [*Turns to* TAMATA] Looking forward to the rest of the fight?

TAMATA: Fuckin' right a am.

OLD RINTY: In the seventh round I was beginning d'wonder what all the talk was about Paterson bein' weakened tryin' d'make the weight. He was supposed d'have starved himself, spent hours in a Turkish Bath, you name it. Accordin' d'all the talk—

TAMATA: All Rinty has d'do is blow on 'im!

OLD RINTY: Instead, he was comin' at me like a pint-sized Cuchulain. I had d'dig deep.

COMMENTATOR: Paterson has forced Monghan back onto the ropes, Monaghan is back-peddling ... ohh!—Paterson is down ... caught with a beautiful right hand ... Monaghan sprints to a neutral corner ... [OLD RINTY *swishes across stage, waltzing with* COLETTE. *An orchestra playing* 'Roisin Dubh' *is heard at high volume.*] The World Champion is down. Jackie Paterson is on the floor ... he looks very groggy ... he's up, he's up and Monaghan darts in ... he catches Paterson with a right, a left, another right ... the pounding is merciless ... he's down, he's down again, and this time it looks like the end ... it is, it is ... and Rinty Monaghan is the new Flyweight Champion of the World!

[OLD RINTY *is dancing with* COLETTE. YOUNG RINTY *appears at the upstairs window of his home. Fade* 'Roisin Dubh'. YOUNG RINTY *is singing* 'When Irish Eyes Are Smiling'. *The crowd joins in for a climactic finish.* YOUNG RINTY *stands at centre stage. A stream of people parade up to him. The first man shakes Young Rinty's hand warmly.*]

FIRST MAN: Well done, Rinty, brilliant. Y'did us all proud.

MRS. GRAHAM: Smashin' Rinty, didn't I tell ye it would be the seventh?

YOUNG RINTY: Y'did indeed, Mrs. Graham.

POLICEMAN: Well done, Rinty.

BARRISTER: A very good show, Rinty. I enjoyed the fight immensely.

DOCKER: Y'bully Rinty, put it there mate.

BUSINESSMAN: So, Rinty, if you just sign here, that ties it up. Rinty Monaghan will advertise Cable Shoes of Ann Street for the next twelve months. [RINTY *signs.*]

YOUNG RINTY: Mrs. Caulfield, whadaya doin' here?

MRS. CAULFIELD: A know you have d'take a break from your trainin', but y'can't do without your goat's milk!

[*She hands* RINTY *two bottles of goat's milk.*]

YOUNG RINTY: Terrific, Mrs. Caulfield, terrific.

[TWO WORKMEN *enter and carry a large new mattress across stage.* ANOTHER MAN *approaches* YOUNG RINTY.]

MATTRESS MAN: There y'go, Rinty. A brand new Dunease mattress, free, courtesy of Robert Dunn and Company.

YOUNG RINTY: Thanks, thanks very much.

REPORTER: Rinty, could y'tell us where your next fight is gonna be?

YOUNG RINTY: No idea, no idea.

REPORTER: Do you know who it's gonna be?

YOUNG RINTY: Haven't a clue.

COALMAN: Well done, Rinty oul' son.

YOUNG RINTY: Right, Tommy, thanks.

PENSIONER: Good on ye, Rinty.

YOUNG RINTY: What about ye, Geordie?

CHOKE-THE-DOG: Could a speak d'ya a minute, Rinty?

YOUNG RINTY: Certainly, Choke-the-dog

CHOKE-THE-DOG: When's your next fight?

YOUNG RINTY: Haven't a clue. Why?

CHOKE-THE-DOG: Will y'be worth backin'?

YOUNG RINTY: I'm always worth backin'.

CHOKE-THE-DOG: That's good. 'Cause the winter's comin' in [*mumbling as he walks off*] nigh and we're lyin' at nights without a fuckin' blanket between us!

[FRANCES *enters and links onto Young Rinty's arm.*]

FRANCES: C'mon, are y'goin' in?

YOUNG RINTY [*looks at watch*]: I thought y'weren't comin'.

FRANCES: A'm only outta work. What's on the night anyway?

YOUNG RINTY: *The Boy With the Green Hair.* Pat O'Brien and Robert Ryan.

FRANCES: Great, c'mon.

YOUNG RINTY: Waita minute, waita minute. Let the crowds get in.

FRANCES: What?

YOUNG RINTY: Let the crowds get in, or there'll be autograph books everywhere.

FRANCES: Who do you think you are, the Pope?

YOUNG RINTY: Right, over here, nigh keep it quiet. [*They approach kiosk*] Two d'the stalls please?

CASHIER: Two d'the stalls. That'll be ... ach hello, Rinty! How y'doin'? You were great against yer man Paterson. Look who it is, Annie—Rinty Munegin!

[YOUNG RINTY *and* FRANCES *hurry into the darkened cinema.*]

FRANCES: I'd be safer comin' d'the pictures with the Invisible Man.

YOUNG RINTY: Shushhhh. Keep it quiet, the picture's startin'.

[*They settle down for a moment and prepare to watch the film. A man arrives behind them, pokes his head in between theirs.*]

MUGS: Hiya, Rinty. Wouldn't sign that wee autograph book for the childer, would ye?

YOUNG RINTY: Certainly.

[MUGS *turns and shouts*]

MUGS: Sambo! Willie! Over here, it's Rinty Munegin! Honest d'frig, a swear. He's sittin' here right beside me. [FRANCES *buries her face.*] Write on it—[*thinks*]—To wee Joseph, undefeated World Champ.

YOUNG RINTY [*repeating as he writes*]**:** To wee Joseph, undefeated ...

[YOUNG RINTY *stops, unsure. He turns to* FRANCES.] Spell undefeated?

OLD RINTY: What did people expect? A left school at twelve. A've had d'pass a lotta difficult tests in my life but a spellin' exam wasn't one a them. Yes, it was fame at last. Not d'mention the money. It wasn't long before a found out one very important thing. It's easier for a wealthy man d'have lots a money than for an ordinary workin' man d'suddenly come across it. M'da saw things I didn't see.

[YOUNG RINTY *and his* DA *enter.* DA *is sitting on an armchair.* YOUNG RINTY *is flashily dressed, ready to go out for the evening.*]

YOUNG RINTY: C'mon da. It's only for a few hours. A'll get y'drunk and get y'home.

DA: No, Rinty son, leave it the night. A'm not feelin' the best.

YOUNG RINTY: The marra night then?

DA: Yiss, yiss, definitely the marra night. And never mind this business of 'you'll get me drunk', I have m'own money. I worked all m'days. [YOUNG RINTY *smiles good humouredly.*] Y'might be champion a the world with a few shillins in your tail, but I'm your da.

YOUNG RINTY: See whada mean, see whada mean? No matter what I say nigh, everybody takes it up wrong. If a wasn't offerin' y'out, a'd be a mangy so-and-so.

DA: Ach, a don't mean it that way, a'm only havin' ye on. Where y'goin' anyway?

YOUNG RINTY: Bangor.

DA: Bangor? What in the name a Jasis ...?

YOUNG RINTY: A've gone inda a wee bit a business out there and a'm goin' down d'see the man that's runnin' it.

DA: What sorta business?

YOUNG RINTY: A dancehall.

DA: Jasis, Mary and St. Joseph!

YOUNG RINTY: It's a good move, da. A have d'put m'money inda something and a dancehall's as good as anything.

DA: A dancehall! Jasis, y'must think yiv money d'burn.

YOUNG RINTY: You know frig all about it.

DA: I know plenty. I've seen the people runnin'd'your door. Complete strangers, half a them. 'Rinty lend is this, lend is that.' You think I'm blind?

YOUNG RINTY: It's my money.

DA: What money? Sure y'haven't earned that much.

YOUNG RINTY: A'm doin' alright.

DA: What? Sure b'the time McAloran takes his whack, y'pay your expenses and the taxman comes along, you'll be wonderin' where your money went.

YOUNG RINTY: Give it a rest, da. A told ye, a'm doin' alright. And anyway, this dancehall's jammed d'the door every weekend. It's a wee goldmine.

DA: Do you count the takins every night?

YOUNG RINTY: Whad are y'on about?

DA: If you're not there d'count the takin's every night, it'll be a goldmine alright—for somebody else.

YOUNG RINTY: I know the man personally. He's a good friend a mine.

DA: Why haven't y'bought yourself a house?

YOUNG RINTY: A'm thinkin' about it.

DA: Thinkin' about it? Y'live in a house that isn't the size a the stable the King keeps one horse in, and you're thinkin' about it.

YOUNG RINTY: I'm buyin' a pub.

[DA *stops abruptly and looks at* YOUNG RINTY.]

DA: That's the first sensible thing yiv said all night.

[*The two men burst out laughing.* DA *gets up and puts his arm around Young Rinty's shoulders.*]

DA: Y'luckin' a bar manager? Are y'serious, buyin' a pub?

YOUNG RINTY: A have an estate agent checkin' a few out not far from here.

DA: All jokin' aside Rinty, it's something like a pub—with you runnin' it and countin' the money every night—that would see you and your wee childer alright in the future. Forget bloody dancehalls.

YOUNG RINTY: So you're not goin' out?

DA: The marra night. Me and you and the oul' woman'll go up d'the Sheridan the marra night.

YOUNG RINTY: Right, c'mon a'll show ya m'new car. [*They move to exit.*]

DA: What?

YOUNG RINTY: A bought a new car.

DA: A holy Jasis, here he goes agin.

YOUNG RINTY: A white Vauxhall. It's the length a three houses.

DA: You can't buy an ordinary black car. It has d'be white? Where d'ya think this is, Hollywood?

YOUNG RINTY: Give over will ye? We're only here once. Why skunk along in back alleyways when y'can walk down the main street?

DA: What are y'talkin' about?

YOUNG RINTY: The difference between black and white, da. I'm not gonna live m'life in the dark.

DA: You're goin' round the bloody ben'.

[YOUNG RINTY *bursts out laughing.*]

YOUNG RINTY: A'm not, a'm goin' d'Bangor. Did a tell ye, 'ave bought four greyhounds?

OLD RINTY: In the summer of 1949, a don't think a was goin' round the bend. As a matter of fact, I reckoned I was sitting pretty— flyin'—maybe even as high as an eagle. A'd won the world title, fought a few other warm-ups and defended m'title once against a tough Frenchman called Maurice Sandeyron. In between, m'first and only son, Sean, was born, and then it was on to a Cockney barra boy by the name of Terry Allen and another defence of m'title. A got down d'some hard trainin' with m'two chief sparrin' partners, Peter Robinson and young Eddie McCullough.

[YOUNG RINTY *and* EDDIE *enter and begin some vigorous joint floor exercises.* YOUNG RINTY *counts aloud.*]

YOUNG RINTY: Ninety-three, ninety-four, ninety-five, ninety-six, ninety-seven, ninety-eight, ninety-nine, a hunderd.

[*They stop, exhausted. They stand up and rub each other down with towels.*]

EDDIE: Fourteen more days d'go.

YOUNG RINTY: Are y'worried?

EDDIE: No, no. But it's my biggest fight yet. If I lose this one—

YOUNG RINTY: Y'won't lose. What did I tell you oul' James said about ye? He says, 'Eddie McCullough's the best prospect he's ever seen in his life.'

EDDIE: Doesn't say much for you.

YOUNG RINTY: He said 'prospect'.

EDDIE: A got a bollockin' of Oul' James the other night.

YOUNG RINTY: What for?

EDDIE: Wants me d'give up the violin.

YOUNG RINTY: Don't heed them. Frank tries d'stop me singin'.

EDDIE: He threatened me. Said it was one or the other or—out!

YOUNG RINTY [*jibing*]: Did you not tell him we all 'need' music?

EDDIE: With Oul' James, a think boxin' is his music. The sight of a boxer landin' one planned punch sets off an orchestra in Oul' James' head. Rinty Munegin's footwork probably sends a hundred violins soarin' round McAloran's Gym.

YOUNG RINTY: Just as long as Eddie McCullough's not playin' one a them.

EDDIE: Yeah.

YOUNG RINTY: You're not gonna give the violin up, are ya?

EDDIE: A've made up m'mind. A have to

YOUNG RINTY: You're mad, Eddie.

EDDIE: You did it, Rinty, and I'm gonna do it. I'm gonna be World Champion.

OLD RINTY: In McAloran's Gym it was widely believed that young Eddie would indeed be a future World Champ. But, just as the were with me, the Mc Alorans weren't sure about his commitment. He played the violin. While his mates were into Glen Miller and Frank Sinatra, young Eddie was into Beethoven and Rossini. And he loved the opera *Carmen*. When we did Boxin' exhibitions up and down the country, I would get up and sing then Eddie would play the violin. Crowd loved it.

YOUNG RINTY: I've a good idea. When I beat Terry Allen you get inda the ring with your violin and back me up.

EDDIE: Y'Jokin'.

YOUNG RINTY: No. I could learn the words of that one you're always playin'—whadaya call it—the Opera?

EDDIE: *Carmen*?

YOUNG RINTY: Yiss. [*Singing*] 'Da da da da'.

YOUNG RINTY and **EDDIE** [*singing*]: 'Da da da da Da da da da, da da da da'.

YOUNG RINTY: Definitely, that's the ticket.

EDDIE: Rinty, I think a few slates have fell outta your roof.

OLD RINTY: Then days before me and Eddie was d'share the Terry Allen bill—tragedy struck.

BUBBLY DAN [*shouting across stage*]: Hey Rinty! [YOUNG RINTY *turns.*] Did y'hear the news? Eddie McCullough's dead!

OLD RINTY: Apparently, he was paintin' the railins of the Mater Hospital when he felt severe pains in his stomach. Within minutes he was in the hospital and a couple a days later—poor Eddie was dead. Peritdonitis. Twenty one years of age. First time a cried since a was a child. Then a had d'pick m'self up and go and fight Terry Allen. And a wasn't without m'own problems.

[DOCTOR *enters, carrying negatives. He speaks to* YOUNG RINTY.]

DOCTOR: I'm afraid the news isn't good Mister Monaghan. Your breathing difficulties are for a very good reason. We've discovered a shadow on your left lung.

YOUNG RINTY: What does that mean?

DOCTOR: Probably the end of your boxing career.

[DOCTOR *exits and* FRANK MCALORAN *enters.*]

FRANK: Won't cancel it, says it's too close d'the fight.

YOUNG RINTY: That's okay, I'm ready, Frank.

FRANK: The doctor says no.

YOUNG RINTY: The doctor isn't me. I need the money. And speakin' of money, call Gardiner in here til we get sorted out what I'm gettin' paid.

FRANK [*moving to exit*]: It's all fixed up. Bob! Bob, would y'come in for a minute?

[BOB GARDINER *enters.*]

BOB: Well, what's the decision Rinty?

YOUNG RINTY: Y'can tell them it's on —

BOB: Ah great, great—

YOUNG RINTY: But only if the agreed financial arrangements apply.

BOB: I've already told Frank. We've signed the contract for £7,000 and you get another six under the counter. Isn't that what we talked about?

YOUNG RINTY: Thanks, Bob.

BOB: Shake on it. [BOB *and* YOUNG RINTY *shake hands and smile happily.*]

OLD RINTY: In spite of the breathin' problems a fought a draw with Terry Allen—I thought a won it. But, that was d'be the last time Rinty Monaghan ever entered the ring again. I retired in April 1950 at the age of 31. What next? I'd no idea. One thing about this existence, y'never know what's comin' next.

[FRANCES *enters in housecoat, slippers, etc. It is early morning, she is bleary-eyed and yawning. She walks across to Colette's bed.*]

FRANCES: Colette. Colette, c'mon love, time d'get up. [COLETTE *doesn't respond.*] What's wrong, love? C'mon, everybody else is up ages ago. Colette? [*She suddenly sees that something is wrong. She leans over and touches the child.*] Colette? What's wrong? Why y'not movin'? What's wrong? [FRANCES *shouts*] Rinty! Rinty, c'mere quick. [YOUNG RINTY *rushes in.*] There's something wrong with Colette, she's wide awake but she's not movin'.

YOUNG RINTY: Let me see. [YOUNG RINTY *touches the child.*] What is it love, c'mon get up. It's brekkie time, c'mon love.

FRANCES [*close to tears*]: God Rinty, there's something wrong with my child.

YOUNG RINTY: Waita minute, waita minute Frances ...

FRANCES [*crying*]: We'll have d'get a doctor.

[FRANCES *wails*]

OLD RINTY: It was a long time and hours of hospital tests and visits by all sorts a doctors before we knew what was wrong.

[DOCTOR *enters.*]

DOCTOR: It's been confirmed, Mister Monaghan. [YOUNG RINTY *and* FRANCES *stare into space.*] Polio. There's been an outbreak. We're dealing with several cases. I'm sorry. [DOCTOR *exits.*]

OLD RINTY: No boxer ever hit me as hard as that doctor did that day. Frances was devastated.

FRANCES: Maybe we shoulda moved house. Maybe it was something she caught in that oul' house ...

YOUNG RINTY: Maybe I should have ...

[*There is silence.*]

OLD RINTY: Even though the doctors explained to us that polio struck at random, our sense of guilt and failure was for long periods, absolute. Sometimes when I brought my four-year-old baby her breakfast in bed, I had to fight hard not to let her see me cryin'. She just smiled and smiled, her beautiful big bright eyes lookin' up at me, so innocent. [OLD RINTY *is close to tears.*] I would be drivin' the car—just drivin' along and suddenly I would burst out cryin'.

[*He is now silently crying. His body shakes slightly. Young Rinty's does the same. They quickly recover.*]

The amazing thing was—[*He smiles*]—as Colette grew up, she showed more fire and guts than the whole lot of us put together. Yes, 1950 was a bad year all round. Retirement, Colette's illness—and as a shoulda known—the promised, under-the-counter payment of six thousand didn't materialise. Funny thing is, I liked Bob Gardiner. But shortly after that he suddenly disappeared outta Belfast and turned up in London, where he spent the rest of his days. Me? I was walkin' along North Queen Street one day when somebody called me from the other side a the street.

[YOUNG RINTY *enters. A man calls him.*]

JIM: Rinty! Rinty!

[YOUNG RINTY *stops and turns.*]

YOUNG RINTY: Hiya Jim, hiya doin'?

JIM: Great. Listen Rinty, I've been luckin' for you.

YOUNG RINTY: What's the problem?

JIM: It's not a problem, it's a proposition.

YOUNG RINTY: Fire away.

JIM: A was readin' in the papers you're retired nigh.

YOUNG RINTY: Doctor says if a throw anor punch, m'left lung'll fall outta m'arse.

OLD RINTY: Jim Reagan was Secretary of the Musicians' Union and one of the best alto-saxophone players in the country.

JIM: A'm startin' a new band. Fancy singin' with us?

YOUNG RINTY: Do I fancy singin' with your new band? Excuse me a second.

[YOUNG RINTY *turns, walks a few paces and jumps in the air, thrusting his fist and whooping. He stops abruptly and returns to* JIM.]

YOUNG RINTY: When do I start?

JIM: As soon as I get the band together and rehearse. There's a ... there's only one problem Rinty?

YOUNG RINTY: What's that?

JIM: A need money d'put the band on the road.

YOUNG RINTY: There's always a catch.

JIM: Yeah, but hold on Rinty, I have it all worked out. The band will be yours. You put the money up and the band'll be yours. I'll look after the music side. A've even got the name an'all. 'Rinty & The Rintonions'. Y'see Rinty, you're famous nigh, w'have d'cash in on your name. We'll clean up. Whadaya say?

YOUNG RINTY: 'Rinty & The Rintonions'?

JIM: That's it.

YOUNG RINTY: Desperate bloody name, Jim.

JIM: Call it 'Rinty & The Buck Eejits' for all I care! Are y'interested?

YOUNG RINTY: A regiment a Jackie Patersons wouldn't stop me.

OLD RINTY [*sarcastically*]: And the legend 'Rinty & The Rintonions' was born. We played all over Ireland—mainly the South. A'll never forget the night we broke the attendance record at Cork City Hall.

[JIM REAGAN *leads the band playing Alto-Sax. Another plays guitar while* BILLY BURNS *plays Double-Bass. The song is* 'Bye Bye Blues'. JIM REAGAN *steps forward to the microphone.*]

JIM: Ladies and gentlemen! The moment you've all been waiting for! The man who defeated Dado Marino! The man who beat Terry Allen! The man who knocked out the great Jackie Paterson! Ladies and gentlemen—from Belfast, the undefeated Flyweight Champion of the World—Rinty Monaghan!

[YOUNG RINTY *enters to loud cheers and applause. He sings a couple of verses of* 'Bye Bye Blues'. *Then he steps forward and lets off a flurry of punches into the air. The crowd cheers wildly. Then as the drummer hits the cymbal* YOUNG RINTY *goes into a tap-dance routine. At the end the crowd cheer and applaud. Next, he does a shadow-boxing, foot-work routine. In the middle of this,* BILLY BURNS *lays down his Double-Bass, takes his glasses off and approaches* YOUNG RINTY, *as though he were a boxing opponent. The two men square up to each other.* BILLY *stretches out his arm and places the palm of his hand on Young Rinty's head.* YOUNG RINTY *then swings punches furiously at* BILLY, *all coming short, in the pretence that he can't reach* BILLY. BILLY *laughs at the audience. Then* BILLY *brings his other hand up in a closed fist and slams it against his hand placed on Young Rinty's head.* YOUNG RINTY *staggers backwards. The music slows in tempo, in time with his staggered movements. When he recovers and begins sparring with* BILLY *again, the music resumes its normal tempo.* YOUNG RINTY *dances around* BILLY *a few times, throwing flurries of punches before* BILLY *returns to his Bass* YOUNG RINTY *finishes the song. The crowd cheer and applaud.*

JIM REAGAN *is putting away his Saxophone. He speaks to the audience.*]

JIM: Rinty had a great presence onstage—charisma. As soon as he came onstage, everybody stopped and listened. He was always in good, chirpy form. A never saw him in bad form once. This was 1950, 1951, and if we were headin' down South for a few days, Rinty would pick us all up in his car. And the first stop before we left Belfast was Musgrave Park Hospital. Rinty had a wee girl, Colette, spendin' a lot a time there and Rinty would bring us all up—the whole band—and we would all say cheerio d'Colette. On the way back it was the same. First stop—Musgrave Park Hospital—and a big pile of presents.

BILLY: Do y'mind the time we opened the Lounge Bar in Ballina?

JIM: The two Guards drunk with us d'six a'clock in the mornin'.

BILLY: Rinty musta sung every song ever fuckin' written that night.

JIM: He just loved singin', loved it.

OLD RINTY: Rinty and the famous Rintonions only lasted 18 months. To this day nobody can remember why we broke up. Another financial disaster. Well, at least a still had m'four greyhounds. And the dancehall.

[young RINTY *is licking an envelope, His daughter* MARTHA, *aged 15, enters.*]

MARTHA: Y'want me, daddy?

YOUNG RINTY: Yiss. A got a message that a friend of mind—know the man runs the dancehall for me? [*She nods*] He's in hospital and wants d'see me. I've d'go away Martha, so I want you d'go up and see the man for me, alright.

[*She nods and takes the envelope. She walks across stage and meets a doctor.*]

MARTHA: A'm here d'see Mister McCall.

DOCTOR: Are you a relative?

MARTHA: No.

DOCTOR: Then I think you'll have to see Mister McCall's relatives before I can speak to you.

[MARTHA *returns to* YOUNG RINTY.]

MARTHA: Daddy?

YOUNG RINTY: Yiss.

MARTHA: The man's dead.

YOUNG RINTY: What?

MARTHA: The man that runs the dancehall for ya is dead. He died 15 minutes before I got d'the hospital.

MARTHA [*to audience*]: M'Daddy went down d'Bangor d'see what was left. He came away with two amplifiers and a microphone stand.

MARTHA: What's wrong, daddy?

YOUNG RINTY: Nothin' love, there's nothin' wrong.

MARTHA: Did that man have money b'longed d'you?

YOUNG RINTY: Nigh Martha, you know that's none of your business.

[MARTHA *stops, looks at the ground, then back to her father.*]

MARTHA: Daddy, have you no money left?

YOUNG RINTY: Of course a have.

MARTHA: Then why are y'always in bad form recently?

YOUNG RINTY: I'm not. I'm not in bad form.

MARTHA: Y'are. Y'can't hide it from us. Y'shouted at Colette yesterday and you don't shout at Colette. Y'shout at us but everybody knows y'don't shout at Colette.

YOUNG RINTY: Is that right?

MARTHA: My friends all think we're millionaires. Every time your photo appears in the papers or your name's mentioned on the radio, everbody thinks, 'Rinty Munegin's doin' very well, isn't he?' You're not a millionaire, daddy, sure you're not?

OLD RINTY: Earnin' money among people who were basically in poverty didn't make it easy. It's a bit like splashin' about in the water after a boat has sunk and you're the only one can swim. Everybody's strugglin' and tryin' d'hold on d'the swimmer, until you're surrounded and strugglin' just like everybody else.

YOUNG RINTY: No Martha, a'm not a millonaire.

OLD RINTY: It's hard d'explain how bad a felt when a realised m'own

15 year old daughter could see so much. A was so fed up that day a headed straight for the Tin Hut, a place where the hardened gamblers among us even played right through the night.

[*Men sit at a table.* OLD RINTY *joins them. They are playing pontoon.* YOUNG RINTY *is banker, dealing out cards.*]

YOUNG RINTY: Right lads, lets have yiz. Any card a painter, just turn it up.

JOE: Here. [*He turns up his card.*]

YOUNG RINTY: Any more? Right, place your bets.

[*The men place their bets—all paper money.*]

JOE: Five spot.

ARCHIE: Two quid.

[YOUNG RINTY *covers their bets.*]

JOE: Deal me a decent card for a change, Rinty, I haven't won since ten a'clock last night.

ARCHIE: Ach, stop moanin'.

JOE: It's alright for you , I'm losin' thirty quid.

ARCHIE: Rinty's losin' a lot more than that.

JOE: He can afford it.

ARCHIE: Much y'down, Rinty?

YOUNG RINTY: Ninety.

JOE: Sure don't worry, y'can always go back d'the boxin'.

YOUNG RINTY: Wish a could. Here we go.

[YOUNG RINTY *deals out the second cards.*]

ARCHIE: Anybody got the time?

YOUNG RINTY: Half-nine.

JOE: Half-nine? I came in here at half-nine last night. The wife'll throw me out.

ARCHIE: Whadaya say, we break after this hand, go d'ten a'clock Mass and start back again?

YOUNG RINTY: Suits me.

JOE: I wanna run home and grab a sandwich.

YOUNG RINTY: Joe?

JOE: Sit.

YOUNG RINTY: Archie?

ARCHIE: Twist. [YOUNG RINTY *deals* ARCHIE *a card.*] Sit.

[YOUNG RINTY *turns up his own hand. He studies for a moment.*]

YOUNG RINTY: Twenties or over, wins.

JOE: Twenties! Bout bloody time. [*Scooping his money*]

ARCHIE: Me too, Rinty.

[*Also scoops his money.* YOUNG RINTY *throws the cards down on the table.*]

ARCHIE: How y'fixed, Rinty?

YOUNG RINTY: Bate out.

ARCHIE: Can y'not go home for more?

YOUNG RINTY: Sure you saw last night, a've been home twice already.

ARCHIE: I could lend y'a tenner.

YOUNG RINTY: Could ya?

ARCHIE: No problem.

YOUNG RINTY: Right, c'mon d'we say a few prayers. Maybe Padre
    Pio'll change m'luck.

OLD RINTY: It was embarrassin'. Even m'best friends thought I'd
    more money than what a had. In fact before the 1950s was out,
    a was wrecked. A bought a black taxi and worked from a stand
    in the centre of Belfast. It kept the wolf from the door. It didn't
    keep m'da from yappin'.

    [*Rinty's* DA *is eating pig's feet.* YOUNG RINTY *stands near him.*]

DA: Greyhounds? Y'lost more money on them greyhounds than
    Randolph Hearst lost in the Wall Street crash. No doubt—you
    made a right balls a things.

YOUNG RINTY: A'm goin' d'England.

DA: What for?

YOUNG RINTY: Been offered work.

DA: More drivin' jobs?

YOUNG RINTY: No.

DA: Buildin' sites?

YOUNG RINTY: A've been offered a part in a pantomime in London.

DA: Just suits ye. Did you not tell them you could bloody well write
    it? Your life's been a bloody pantomime.

YOUNG RINTY: It's good money.

DA: Don't talk d'me about good money.

YOUNG RINTY: Da, you don't seem d'understand something. I don't
    live for money. If a have it, great. If a haven't, a'm not gonna
    throw m'self inda the Pollock dock.

DA [*shouting*]: Y'had it! Y'had it! That's what annoys me. Y'had it,
    for frigsake! [*There is silence between the men.*]

YOUNG RINTY: Where's m'ma?

DA: Bingo.

YOUNG RINTY: Where?

DA: The Parish Hall. That reminds me. 'Member that big Charity
    'Do' the Priest asked me d'see you about?

YOUNG RINTY: What ... what one was that?

DA: Y'know, in St. Mary's Hall? They're expectin' the Bishop and

2,000 people at it. Priest asked me d'ask you d'make a guest appearance, givin' out the prizes or something, d'ya mind?

YOUNG RINTY: Is that the one Ruby Murray's singin' at?

DA: The very one.

YOUNG RINTY: When is it?

DA: Ach, y'needin' be botherin'. I told them y'would do it, but the committee has already got Freddie Gilroy.

YOUNG RINTY: What?

DA: He's the current Bantamweight Champion of Europe. Might be fightin' for a World Title soon.

YOUNG RINTY: Might be?

DA: Y'have d'understand their point a view. It's over 12 years since you were World Champion, Rinty. They want whoever's new. The public's very fickle, son. Like Errol Flynn with weemin. He no sooner picked one up, til he was luckin' a new one. Never satisfied. Are y'goin' round d'the pub?

YOUNG RINTY: No. No, not the night, da.

DA: C'mon. It's a good night. Singsong night, but Kirkpatrick won't start the singsong without me. C'mon round and give is a song. The customers'll be glad d'see ya.

YOUNG RINTY [*moving to exit*]: Why don't y'get Freddie Gilroy? [YOUNG RINTY *leaves with* DA *shouting after him.*]

DA: Freddie Gilroy? Sure he couldn't sing d'get himself outta Purgatory! [*Mumbles*] Freddie friggin' Gilroy.

[YOUNG RINTY *walks, disconsolate, to downstage right. He stops and takes a cigarette out. He searches for matches but without success.* OLD RINTY *comes across and offers a lighted match.*]

YOUNG RINTY: Thanks.

OLD RINTY: Waitin' on a bus?

YOUNG RINTY: Yeah.

OLD RINTY: Y'look fed up. [YOUNG RINTY *nods, staring straight ahead.*] No big white car, nigh.

[YOUNG RINTY *looks at him puzzled.*]

YOUNG RINTY: Do I know you?

OLD RINTY: Not yet, no.

YOUNG RINTY: Not yet?

OLD RINTY: Yiv time enough. Another 21 years exactly.

YOUNG RINTY: What d'hell are you on about?

OLD RINTY: You're Rinty Monaghan, right?

YOUNG RINTY: That's right.

OLD RINTY: So am I.

[YOUNG RINTY *looks closer, more quizzically, at* OLD RINTY.]

YOUNG RINTY: Are you nuts?

OLD RINTY: No.

YOUNG RINTY: Nuts come up to me all the time. You're a nut.

OLD RINTY: A'm not. I'm Rinty Monaghan. I'm you.

[YOUNG RINTY *looks at* OLD RINTY. *He turns away and looks at his watch.*]

YOUNG RINTY: Where's this bloody bus?

OLD RINTY: Y'don't believe me?

YOUNG RINTY: Give my head pace mate, will ya?

OLD RINTY: Ask me something? [YOUNG RINTY *looks at him.*] Ask me something about yourself and I'll prove to ya that I'm you.

[YOUNG RINTY *shifts around a little.*]

YOUNG RINTY: What was my mother's name?

OLD RINTY: Martha. She was a Protestant from Glasgow Street off York Street. She became a convert. [YOUNG RINTY *looks at him suspiciously.*]

YOUNG RINTY: What did m'da buy me for m'fifteenth birthday?

OLD RINTY: A trumpet. It split m'lip and a had d'give it up because of the boxin'.

YOUNG RINTY: Whadaya mean you had d'give it up? I'm talkin' about me.

OLD RINTY: So am I.

YOUNG RINTY: You're beginnin' d'annoy me, mate. [*Silence*] You reckon you're me, then? [OLD RINTY *nods.*] Then how come you're that age?

OLD RINTY: You'll have d'work that one out for yourself.

YOUNG RINTY: If you know all about my past—and you're that age— a suppose you think you know something about my future?

OLD RINTY: Everything.

YOUNG RINTY: Go and bollicks.

OLD RINTY: Try me?

YOUNG RINTY: Well, what happens next?

OLD RINTY: Well, a can't remember exactly what time this bus came at but—

YOUNG RINTY: Y'know rightly whada mean—this year, next year, what happens?

OLD RINTY: A went d'London, did a very successful pantomime, had a great time.

YOUNG RINTY: I'm booked d'do a pantomime!

OLD RINTY: Then a did a smashin' tour of Variety Halls, singin' all over Britain. Glasgow, Liverpool, Birmingham.

YOUNG RINTY: I've boxed in all them places.

OLD RINTY: Oh—and a trained the Showbiz Football team. Lonnie Donnegan, Bernard Bresslaw, that mob.

YOUNG RINTY: Really?

OLD RINTY: Knocked about with Billy Wright a good deal—know the footballer—married d'one of the Beverly Sisters? Great fella.

YOUNG RINTY: I'd love d'do all that.

OLD RINTY: Y'did do it.

YOUNG RINTY: Then what happened?

OLD RINTY: Well, basically a was an immigrant. A homesick immigrant. A wanted d'go home.

YOUNG RINTY: Y'silly shite.

OLD RINTY: Ah, a've no regrets. England was good, but there's no feelin' replaces bein' among your own. Strange thing was, in England a was treated as a celebrity, taken b'the hand. It was the same in Dublin, but Belfast? ... a was just Rinty Munegin from Little Corporation Street.

YOUNG RINTY: But I wanna leave Belfast because a can't get decent work.

OLD RINTY: Well, when a came back a got a job with a big car company. The told me a would mostly be doin' Public Relations and a 'bit a drivin'.' Turned out a spent the next ten years drivin' a lorry over every bloody road that ever existed. The closest a got d'Public Relations was drivin' past the *Belfast Telegraph* offices on m'way outta Belfast every week.

YOUNG RINTY: Do y'mean, y'ended up drivin' a lorry?

OLD RINTY: Yiss. You end up drivin' a lorry.

YOUNG RINTY: Not me, mate. The singin' in England bit and knockin' about with Billy Wright and Lonnie Donnegan, yis, but there's no way a'm gonna spend ten years drivin' a lorry.

OLD RINTY: What about a petrol-pump attendant?

YOUNG RINTY: What?

OLD RINTY: A packed in the lorry-drivin' and spent the last years of m'life workin' as a petrol-pump attendant.

YOUNG RINTY: Good luck d'ya mate, but I think you were a friggin' eejit.

OLD RINTY: A used d'rise every mornin' at six and open the garage. Then something happened. A man called Charlie Tosh pulled in for petrol one day.

CHARLIE: Five pounds, please.

[CHARLIE *hands* OLD RINTY *money.* OLD RINTY *searches pockets for change.*]

CHARLIE [*Coleraine accent*]: You Rinty Monaghan?

OLD RINTY: Used d'be. [*Laughs*]

CHARLIE: I heard you singin' years ago, out in Coleraine.

OLD RINTY: Y'probably did.

CHARLIE: How's it goin'?

OLD RINTY: Ach, alright. Can't complain, can't complain. Nobody listens anyway. [*Laughs*] Five pounds. [*Hands* CHARLIE *his money*]

CHARLIE: Doin' any singin' these days?

OLD RINTY: Not a'tall. The wife doesn't even let me talk, never mind sing. [*Laughs*]

CHARLIE: Well, good meetin' y'Rinty.

OLD RINTY: And you too.

CHARLIE: Listen, I've a fireplace business round the corner there, call in anytime for an oul' yarn.

OLD RINTY: Will do, will do.

CHARLIE: Good luck.

OLD RINTY: All the best.

CHARLIE: Rinty did call in and after a while, me and him got very friendly. He started sellin' fireplaces for me! That's right. Rinty would be in the shop havin' a yarn and a cup of coffee and he would go over to a customer and tell them how good such and such a fireplace was. Laughin' and jokin', y'know. Most of the customers knew who he was and before y'knew it, he'd sold a couple of fireplaces. But, the other side of things, is that I run a wee independent record company called Hawk Records, and for months I coaxed Rinty d'come inda the studio and record his famous boxin' anthem. He wouldn't hear tell of it. 'I'm 64,' he kept sayin. But I never gave up.

[*Recording studio.* OLD RINTY *with headphones on is singing at a microphone.* CHARLIE TOSH *and* KATHY *are listening.* OLD RINTY *is singing* 'When Irish Eyes Are Smiling' *to a pre-recorded soundtrack. The song comes to an end.*]

RECORDING ENGINEER [*tannoy*]: That's it. Well done, Rinty. Y'can go for a drink nigh.

OLD RINTY: It's not a drink a need, it's an injection.

CHARLIE: That was great, Rinty.

OLD RINTY: A wonder will the let me on *Top of the Pops*.

KATHY: I'd buy it.

CHARLIE: Rinty, a hope d'release it within two months, then a have a wee suggestion for ye.

OLD RINTY: Aye, 'Piss off, Rinty'.

CHARLIE: No, no. I'm puttin' together a tour of the Eileen Donaghy Show. A want you d'close the first half.

OLD RINTY: If y'have me on it, I'll close the whole bloody show.

KATHY: We'll provide transport and get y'home safely every night, Mister Monaghan.

CHARLIE: Seriously, Rinty, would y'do it?

OLD RINTY: Seriously Charlie, no. My days of singin' are over. Who knows Rinty Monaghan nighadays?

[*Black-out. Concert stage. Spotlight on* OLD RINTY *singing* 'I'm Always Chasing Rainbows'. *The audience applaud and cheer.* CHARLIE TOSH *enters and puts his arm around Old Rinty's shoulder.*]

CHARLIE: Well done, Rinty, well done. Another great show. They love ya.

OLD RINTY: Do you think so?

CHARLIE: Do I think so? Rinty, you've been so popular on this tour that I've already organised another, bigger one. And it's gonna be *The Rinty Monaghan Show*. You'll be top of the bill, Rinty.

OLD RINTY: Charlie, I need to talk to you.

CHARLIE: And I need d'talk d'you. Where have you always wanted d'visit?

OLD RINTY: A need d'visit the loo right now.

CHARLIE: But where were you always bein' invited to box when you were World Champion, but never made it?

OLD RINTY: The States, but Charlie—

CHARLIE: It's all arranged. After y'do the next tour in the autumn, we go on a tour of the United States for six full weeks, eh?

[RINTY *tries to look pleased. He turns his face away, his mind on other thoughts.*]

CHARLIE: Whadaya say, Rinty?

OLD RINTY: Charlie, I need d'talk d'you.

CHARLIE: Go ahead.

OLD RINTY: A wanna thank you for all yiv done for me.

CHARLIE: Don't be ridiculous. It's you's givin' me the pleasure.

OLD RINTY: No, honestly, Charlie, what you've done for me this last lotta months, I couldn't repay you.

CHARLIE: You're talkin' through your hat. You're bringin' payin' customers through the door.

OLD RINTY: It's all because of you. I'm out there on that stage hearin' the applause again—because of you.

CHARLIE: Wait til we get d'America!

OLD RINTY: That's what a wanna talk d'you about.

CHARLIE: And wait till y'hear this. This is the big one. Y'listenin'? [OLD RINTY *is uninterested.*] After six months of protracted negiations—Eamon Andrews—you've heard of Eamon Andrews? [OLD RINTY *nods*.] Eamon Andrews has agreed d'have Rinty Monaghan on *This Is Your Life*!

OLD RINTY: You're a spoof.

CHARLIE: It's true. A have all the letters. Signed, sealed and delivered. He's sendin' a researcher over after Christmas.

[OLD RINTY *shakes his head, bewildered. He is confused, saddened.*]

OLD RINTY: Charlie, I haven't been doin' too well recently—

CHARLIE: You're a diabetic. We can handle that, I'll pay for all the medicine y'need.

OLD RINTY: No, it's worse than that.

CHARLIE: Whadaya mean?

OLD RINTY: A developed gland trouble around the throat and the sent me for more tests. [*Pause*] They've discovered cancer.

CHARLIE: Really? Christ, Rinty.

OLD RINTY: How far it's gone or how much there is, the don't know at the minute, but ...

CHARLIE: I'm very sorry d'hear that, Rinty.

OLD RINTY: Well, there is one thing a wanna say. A'm gonna fight it. Yiv give me too much d'live for, Charlie.

CHARLIE: It's nothin' d'do with me, Rinty. It's you. You're Rinty Monaghan, not me.

[YOUNG RINTY *enters.*]

YOUNG RINTY: What did you say there?

CHARLIE: A said, 'He's Rinty Monaghan, not me.'

OLD RINTY: Believe me, nigh?

YOUNG RINTY: Yeah, and a don't know whether d'laugh or cry.

OLD RINTY: Why, whats wrong?

YOUNG RINTY: You

OLD RINTY: What about me?

YOUNG RINTY: Luck at ye.

OLD RINTY: What's wrong with me?

YOUNG RINTY: Luck at the state of ya.

OLD RINTY: Hey boy, don't you get cheeky w'me.

YOUNG RINTY: But why did y'do it?

OLD RINTY: Do what?

YOUNG RINTY: Y'ended up a petrol pump attendant.

OLD RINTY: It wasn't a bad wee job, it was close d'the house. Listen son ... [OLD RINTY *approaches* YOUNG RINTY, *remonstrating. He places his hand on Young Rinty's shoulder.*]... It wasn't easy d'get jobs ...

[YOUNG RINTY *pushes Old Rinty's hand off and grabs him by the lapels.*]

YOUNG RINTY: But why? Why? [*He shakes* OLD RINTY. OLD RINTY *struggles and frees himself.*] I did things. I achieved things. I worked my balls off. I trained harder than any man alive. I developed my body to the point where a had the strength of ten men. I was Champion of the World. I did all that. What d'fuck are you doin' servin' bloody petrol?

OLD RINTY: Hold on, hold on! Don't shout at me. It wasn't my fault. There was circumstances.

YOUNG RINTY: What circumstances?

OLD RINTY: A whole lotta things.

YOUNG RINTY: Like what?

OLD RINTY: Y'wouldn't understand.

YOUNG RINTY: A don't.

OLD RINTY: But sure things is on the up again. Did y'not see that a've made a new record for Charlie Tosh and a'm out singin again? There's a possible tour of the States and a'm gonna be on *This Is Your Life*. It's all beginnin' d'happen again.

YOUNG RINTY: Aye, when a'm half dead.

OLD RINTY: Who's half dead? A'd go ten rounds w'you, anyday.

YOUNG RINTY: You're an oul' clapped out has-been.

OLD RINTY: It comes to us all.

YOUNG RINTY: Frig it, frig it, frig it.

OLD RINTY: Don't take it so bad. It could be worse. Poor Jackie Paterson was stabbed d'death 25 years ago in a Johannasburg public house. Benny Lynch drunk himself d'death at 33.

YOUNG RINTY: Didn't I hear you say something earlier on about not bein' well?

OLD RINTY: Aye, it's just an oul' complaint a have, not do me a blind bit of harm.

YOUNG RINTY: You're a liar.

OLD RINTY: A'm not.

YOUNG RINTY: What am I gonna die of? [OLD RINTY *remains silent.*] A said, what am I gonna die of?

OLD RINTY: None a your business. What's a young man like you worryin' about your funeral for?

YOUNG RINTY: Tell me!

OLD RINTY: Give my head pace. Away you on and do your pantomime in London. Here, there's a smashin' wee club in Soho run b'a fella called Joe Rosato. Me and him got on like a house on fire. Sleg him about Kate, he'll know what you're on about.

YOUNG RINTY: I don't believe you.

OLD RINTY: What?

YOUNG RINTY: I don't believe you're really me.

OLD RINTY: Holy Jesis.

YOUNG RINTY: Okay, in what fight did I break my right hand?

[CHARLIE *moves downstage.*]

OLD RINTY: Tommy Stewart.

YOUNG RINTY: How did you know that?

OLD RINTY: It was my hand!

CHARLIE: Rinty did indeed have cancer. We started the second tour because he insisted. He was a bundle of nerves goin' on stage. Apart from 'Irish Eyes', his big, closin' number was 'My Way'. Sometimes he would come off-stage after 'My Way'—cryin'— partly because of the fantastic audience reaction, partly because of his own emotions. Other times people would shout up 'What about Jackie Paterson?' or 'What about Dado Marino?' Rinty would laugh his head off and shake his fist at whoever shouted. He relished the recognition, the applause, the adulation. He was a born entertainer. The recording, the tours had given him back all his old confidence and, above all, his self-respect.

But it wasn't long before he was confined to Montgomery House where he underwent fifteen different treatments.

[YOUNG RINTY *takes old* RINTY *by the hand and guides him upstage to a chair. He sits him down and carefully places a blanket across his lap, tucking it in around his waist.* YOUNG RINTY *stands directly behind* OLD RINTY.]

And still he tried to remain cheery. Once, a woman came up to his bed and said she danced with him years ago. Rinty got up in his pyjamas and danced a waltz with the woman up and down the ward with all the other patients and visitors cheerin' and clappin'. That was just Rinty.

[*Melody from* Carmen *fades up to low.* OLD RINTY *feebly raises his face from his chest.*]

OLD RINTY: Is that you, Eddie? Eddie McCullough. How are y'Eddie, son? A see you're still playin' the old 'hey diddle, diddle.' Beautiful, Eddie son, beautiful. A saw m'mother tonight. She was standin' at the end of the bed. She was beautiful, too. Absolutely beautiful. Y'know, y'can go through life and y'can count on the fingers of one hand, how many things are really beautiful. You were right, Eddie. You and Maxie were right. We need music. I shoulda put the music before the boxin'. Boxin's a mug's game. It's excitin' for them that's watchin'. Luck at me. From the top d'the bottom's a long way. From the beginnin'

d'the end's even longer. But at least a was up there ... like an
eagle among birds ... a mountain among hills and ... and king
among men ... a was up there. A can take that d'my grave.
[*Pause*]

   You still there, Eddie? Good. Good. Fancy a couple a rounds?
C'mon. A might be poor but a'm not about d'wrap up just yet.
[*He throws the blankets back and gets out of bed.*] I could still bate
this whole thing, y'know. It's only cancer. It's not Jackie
Paterson. C'mon? C'mon Eddie? [*He begins to move around the
hospital ward, shadow-boxing in pyjamas and bare feet.*] Let's go
Eddie. Let's fly. Play the music, Eddie. Louder! [*He is shouting.
The music builds.*] Eagles. We're eagles. That's it—fly. Beautiful
Eddie, beautiful. [OLD RINTY *is, by now, standing centre stage,
shouting to the heavens at the top of his voice.* Carmen *reaches
crescendo.*]

   C'mon Eddie son, fly!
   Up, up!
   That's it! Like eagles!

The music stops abruptly. Black-out.

WHAT DID I KNOW WHEN I WAS NINETEEN?

What Did I Know When I Was Nineteen? was first performed on 27th October 2000 at the Crumlin Road Courthouse as part of that year's Belfast Festival at Queen's. It was produced as part of a group of seven short plays commissioned by Tinderbox Theatre Company for the production, *Convictions*. The play was produced by Jimmy Fay. The actor was Vincent Higgins.

Author's Notes

Set in the main hallway of Crumlin Road Courthouse, Belfast.

The main character is the GHOST *of a former prisoner who was sentenced to be hanged in the Courthouse sometime around the middle of the twenieth century.*

GHOST *is a very angry, embittered, enraged person who spends most of the monologue giving off at a furious, high-octane, hardly-stopping-for-a-breath, pace.*

He has a speech pattern associated with his emotional state where he will shout out monosyllabic words or phrases at the audience and repeat the same word or phrase, over and over.

Set:
The actor will have the use of four playing areas.
The Balcony, two raised platforms at either side of the main hallway and the floor of the Hallway itself.
On one platform will be the artefacts of family life e.g. a life-size cardboard cut-out photograph of a Belfast working-class family circa 1930s, a table and chair.
The only item on the table is a woman's wedding ring.
The Hangman's Noose will dangle above the other platform.

Hallway of Crumlin Road Courthouse, Belfast. From above the audience on the balcony, an angry voice fills the air. GHOST *is staring down at them. He leans over the balcony, his chest heaving, his eyes on fire. Above another platform on the other side of the hallway, a Hangman's Noose dangles.*

[GHOST *singing soulfully at the top of his voice from Otis Redding's* 'These Arms Of Mine'.]

'These!
These!
These-arms-of-my-i-i-i-ine
They are longing
They are longing
For-or-or-you-oo-oo ... '

[GHOST *abruptly stands to attention as though facing the judge. He barks out the words of a Court Clerk*]

as **COURT CLERK:** Prisoner B2450—please stand to attention!

GHOST: What did I know when I was nineteen? Eh? Tell me what the hell would somebody like me know when I was nineteen? Like, what do I know about anything? All I know is that I know nothin' about nothin'. Molly wouldn't have known much better, either.

Okay, it was good of you to come. Y'wait until the place closes down and all the pain and heartbreak has come and gone, then you turn up, then you turn up, then you turn up, y'shower a bastards. And, behave like a pile of voyeuristic, theatre-goin', fun-seeking, hedonistic, facile assholes.

[*In full view of the audience,* GHOST *climbs down from the balcony onto the floor in the hallway, landing in among the audience. He continues his tirade, on occasion, poking his finger into the faces of audience members.*]

GHOST: I'll tell you what I want to know. Do you know what I want to know? Here's what I want to know. How come, the jails were always filled with the poor people, the poor people, the working man, the labourin' man, the poor uneducated, stupid, no hopin', no hopin', no mouth, no hopin', tongueless, ordinary, stupid, bastard workin' man, eh? As a said, I don't know nothin' about nothin' but I'd love somebody to tell me how in hell did it work out that way? I mean. Am I only imagin' this? Maybe I am. Maybe there was a courthouse and a jail hidden in some other part of Belfast that dealt with all the money people that did wrong, but I just never heard of it. Or maybe money people never do anything wrong. Whatever it is goes on, the one thing we do know for certain—very, very few of them ever ended up bein' paraded through the corridors of this place, handcuffed to a Prison Warder like some kind of animal, some kind of dog, mongrel, monkey, donkey, animal.

[GHOST *takes a run and jumps up on the 'Hangman's' Platform and quickly comes to attention. He speaks as* COURT CLERK.]

as **COURT CLERK:** Prisoner B2450—how do you plead ?

GHOST [*handling the Hangman's Noose.*]: Seventeen men. Seventeen men sentenced in this buildin' and hanged over there since 1854. In other words, a combination of politicians, judges and solicitors— the shirt and tie brigade—killed a man once every six years.

Seventeen men. A combination of vagrants, down and outs, passion killers and republicans—and I knew every one of them.

From the very first man. Private Robert Henry O'Neill. who shot a bullyin' corporal in Victoria Barracks in 1854, to Tom Williams the republican martyr, I knew them all. And the last man—McGladdery from Newry, who killed Pearl Gamble in 1961, because she wouldn't let him leave her home from a dance. He got his dance in the end—with this. [*Indicates the rope*]

Seventeen men. One every six years. Killed by the shirt and tie brigade.

[GHOST *abruptly stands to attention. He speaks as the* COURT CLERK.]

as **COURT CLERK:** Prisoner B2450—please take the stand!

GHOST: Then there was me. Me and Molly. Did you ever come across a girl with a sparkle in her eyes ? Y'know, you actually see something that looks like a spark, dartin' about, bouncin' like mad, doin' a jig, jumpin' for joy, leapin' like a lunatic, cracklin' like billyo, all over her eyes.

[*He jumps down from the Hangman's platform and runs across to the 'Family' platform. He stands to attention.*]

as **COURT CLERK:** Prisoner B2450—please place your right hand on the Bible!

GHOST [*pointing to the artefacts*]: I was of a lowly position in the world. Look at me. How in God's name did I get to this? I lay in my cell night after night and I asked myself that question over and over. Look at me? [*Pause*] What did I know about anything? [*He shouts.*] Family! Some facts.

[**GHOST** *embarks on a routine where he shouts questions to himself and then answers them.*]

BORN?
In a hovel.

WHERE?
In a lovely wee hovel in the lovely, beautiful, bountiful slums of Belfast.

WHEN?
Sometime around the time they launched the Titanic, m'granny was never sure.

PARENTS?
Mother Jeannie, the baby breeder. The stupid, dosy, pitiful, unquestionin, pathetic, one-woman baby-makin' factory. Father, Rab, the non-workin' painter & decorator. The non-workin', non-thinkin', non-worryin', non-carin', leg-over-when-ever-the-fuck-he-liked, silly bastard, painter and decorator.

SCHOOL?

Hardly ever went. Nobody around me ever thought it was important enough. But what was I supposed to know when I was ten?

LOVE?

That, my friends, was the problem. It's why I'm standin' here. When I was just sixteen I fell in love with a girl who worked in a shop beside the Alambra Picture House. Molly—the girl with the sparkle in her eye—I took her to the Alambra in May and she asked me to marry her in June. We got married in January, but what the hell did I know when I was seventeen?

CHILDREN?

Only one child. Poor Sammuel.

WORK?

Started work in a timber yard when I was 13 and then moved to the abattoir. That's where a got the knife, the blade, the dagger, the knife, it was a big knife, a big, big sharp knife.

JAIL?

[GHOST *jumps down from the 'home' platform and places himself in the middle of the Court Hallway.*]

Arrived into this building around about the time the wireless became popular. Used d'pass this building every week on m'way d'play football. Now, I was in it. Right in it. Came in through that door, surrounded. Surrounded by prison warders, big prison warders, peelers, giant peelers, keys, lots and lots of keys, janglin' like hundreds of mini-repetitive threats, solicitors, barristers, arrogant, ignorant, snobby, cheeky aloof solicitors and barristers, big high ceilings, big high doors, the smell of polish, the smell of wood, the feel of authority, the feeling of powerlessness. I felt like a piece of shite. I felt like I was scum. I felt scruffy and dirty beside all the sharp suits and shirts and ties and wigs and briefcases. I felt like everything I was, couldn't be good. There must be something wrong with me. There must be something wrong with who I am. There must be something wrong with where I've come from. There must be something wrong with my mother and father. My family, my district, my friends, myself. How could whoever I was, be any good? I remember even thinkin' a bizarre thought. I thought, 'Why do I not wear a shirt and tie? Why does my father not wear a shirt and tie? If only we wore shirts and ties, everything would be alright. We would be good people just like all these people here. If only we wore shirts and ties.'

[*The* GHOST *charges back up onto the 'family' platform. He comes to attention and speaks as the* COURT CLERK.]

as **COURT CLERK:** Prisoner B2450, do you remember the night in question?

[GHOST *lifts the wedding ring and fingers it. Speaks as himself.*]

GHOST: Jealousy, that's what got me, jealousy, rage, shite, anger, pig-headedness. Stupid friggin' daft, pig-headedness jealousy, that's what got to me. I couldn't stand certain things. Just couldn't let certain things go. Certain things, wee things I thought were big things. M'mind would wonder and it would drive me crazy. Three weeks after she left me I tried to get her back and it all went wrong. I heard about a man. I heard she was seen talkin' to a man. I knew him. She was supposed to be livin' in her mother's and I heard she was seen talkin' to a man I knew. I know now that that's all it was ... but then ... my mind went crazy. I imagined things. I sat on a wall near her mother's house and I imagined things. Little pictures were forcing their way in to my mind. Little dangerous, bastard, painful, bastard, painful, painful, hurtin' pictures. I saw him, this man I knew, I saw him kissin' her. I saw her likin' it. I saw his hand liftin' her dress. Molly smiled. What the hell was she doin' smilin'? I saw his hand running up the outside of her thigh. I saw it as sure as I see you now. I saw his hand tug at her knickers, this was Molly's knickers, he was tuggin' at Molly's knickers, why was he tuggin' at Molly's knickers and why was she lettin' him, why ...

[GHOST *lets out a blood curling scream. He drops violently on to the floor of the platform. Slowly, he recovers. He looks out at the audience and starts to sing.*]

'These lips of mi-i-i-ine
They are burning

They are burning
From wanting you-oo-oo ...   '

What ... what did I know when I was nineteen?

[*He improvises the end of the song à la Otis Redding He sits on the edge of the platform.* GHOST *abruptly scrambles to affention. He speaks now as* JUDGE.]

as **JUDGE:** Prisoner B2450. It only remains for me to pass upon you the sentence of the law, which is that you shall be taken from the place you now stand, back to the jail, that hence, on Friday the 4th of May, you shall be taken to the place of common execution—the gallows—and that you shall be hanged by the neck until you be dead. Your body shall be buried within the precincts of the jail, and may the Lord have mercy on your soul.

[GHOST *races across and jumps up on the 'Hangman's' platform. He begins to check the placing of the noose, it's strength etc. He speaks as himself.*]

GHOST: So. It's been an interesting night. Belfast says goodbye to Crumlin Road Courthouse. The place stank, and it was the Belfast poor who got it right up the nose. It was only solicitors and the like, who will remember the sweet smell of roses. [*Pause*]
      After she was buried I begged my mother to try and get me Molly's wedding ring. I put it in my breast pocket and kept it there, right up until the end.

[GHOST *slowly begins to button up his shirt and put a tie on.*]

They marched me from the condemned cell into the execution chamber next door.

[*He places the rope around his neck and leans into it.*]

The only time I got to wear a shirt and tie in my whole life. Goodnight.

Black-out